What others are saying about *"Journey to Authenticity"*

"In over 25 years since meeting Pastor Sonny Misar, I have met few men with such wise perspective, warm spirit, and positive faith in the Savior and His plan for His people. This rich book reflects the genuine wisdom and love of a spiritual father and mentor. Particularly, if you are in a tough, demanding, discouraging situation...you will be strengthened by reading and applying the truths therein. With Pastor Misar's help you can find 'the sweet center of your true identity in Christ.'"

Pastor John Havener
New Testament Church
Lillian, Alabama

"Sonny Misar's book is a gem. With clarity and sensitivity he charts the journey that most of us will travel. He brings understanding and explanation to the cycles of life that we often plunge into and at a loss to know what to do. *Journey to Authenticity* gives hope and practical steps which will help us successfully negotiate our way through the various stages we are destined to pass. I thoroughly recommend this book and will be giving a copy to all of my colleagues and friends."

Paul Reid
Senior Pastor, Christian Fellowship Church
Belfast, Ireland

"Excellent! To the point, timeless truths that are finally in book form. The principles are Biblical, clear, and hold the attention of the reader. Sonny does a great job shedding light on a topic of vital spiritual importance to the reader. You will learn a lot of things you didn't know before reading this book, and it will provoke you to think... and most importantly, to act!

Rick Iglesias
Senior Pastor, Pleasant Valley Church
Winona, Minnesota

"Sonny Misar does an incredible job of describing the seasons of life we all go through. It is extremely helpful to understand the season of life that you are in, what you have just passed through, and where you are headed. It gives you a sense of security to know that what you are going through is "normal" and to find God in it. I found that this book surprised me as I read it and was fascinated to have my present season of life described so accurately. This is a book that comforts, challenges, and equips. Read it yourself and share it with others.

David Wells
Team leader, Life Links International church network
Regina, Saskatchewan, Canada

"One of the most needed areas where the Church today needs clarity is in the whole arena of spiritual identity and its development. Too often the Church has been vague when it comes to its approach to the development of our growing identity in Christ. That's why I am so eager to endorse this new work by Sonny Misar. Scripturally based and easy to grasp, Sonny's work combines Scriptural clarity with practical insights gleaned from many years of experience as a pastor and leader in the Body of Christ. This work will go a long way in helping God's people understand the stages involved in moving into spiritual maturity. I am happy to recommend it."

Neil Silverberg
Team Leader, Masterbuilders
Cape Coral, Florida

"With a blend of wise spiritual counsel and the illumination of personal experience, the author presents a road map to help make sense of the changing terrain of life's spiritual journey. Reading it you will discover that many of the puzzling or even painful experiences of your life actually came about as part of God's developmental plan for you, his beloved child. I highly recommend this book for personal use and as a gift to other fellow travelers."

Paul F. Koehler, D. Min.
President, King's Commission Ministries, Inc.
Author of *Telling God's Stories with Power*

"This book is a pleasure to commend. It gives clear insight into the development of our spiritual identity. Journey to Authenticity is an interesting and helpful read for anyone wanting to understand God's purposes for the different seasons in life."

Pastor Jim McCracken
Leader of the TrueBridge family of churches
Eden Prairie, Minnesota

"As we journey through life we encounter different stages or seasons and it is God's plan that we would grow spiritually through each of them – that we would gain a greater understanding of who we are in Christ. It has been my experience that not every season has felt like a growth stage, but in "Journey to Authenticity" Sonny Misar, in such a personal and practical way, helps us to see how God is shaping our lives in every season. You'll be encouraged as you read and you'll definitely want to dig deeper into God's plan for your amazing journey."

Dale E. Hewitt
Senior Minister, Dreambuilders Church
Perth, Australia

"I was delighted to read Sonny Misar's book, *Journey to Authenticity* for several reasons. First, it provided great insight concerning the various stages of my own spiritual journey spanning more than 5 decades. Secondly, it gave perspective on my present, on-going quest to allow Christ to live in and through me in a way that impacts those around me. Thirdly, I believe that this work will provide a useful tool in mentoring many in various stages of their own pilgrimage. The scope of the material was awesome, the diversity of quotes from noteworthy personages was refreshing, and the honest, personal-life illustrations were encouraging. I heartily recommend this work to all in ministry and especially to all who are engaged in mentoring and coaching others in life and ministry."

Dr. Frank Harvey
Founder and Bishop of Covenant Life Ministries
Clyde, North Carolina

"It has been said that every point of arrival is a point of departure. Pastor Sonny's book, Journey to Authenticity, has come in due season as a vital resource that not only helps us to understand our location on the journey called life, but to better deal with the realities we face in the process of becoming. Journey to Authenticity is an excellent resource for the explorer-discoverer-learner, at every stage of life and it is as ideal for the beginner, as it is for the seasoned coach, mentor and counsellor. Firmly grounded in God's word and drawing from experience forged in the crucible of life, it offers practical hints, tips and tools and that will help the reader-sojourner to anticipate and avoid the usual pitfalls, make better sense of the sometimes confusing patterns that inevitably arise, and navigate, with greater confidence and assurance, the various stages of spiritual identity development. I wholeheartedly recommend this book."

Emmanuel Mbakwe
National Leader, The Apostolic Church, United Kingdom
London, England

“Sonny Misar graduated with honors from Liberty Christian College, Pensacola, Florida in 1986. During his college career, he was an active member of Liberty Church in Pensacola. It was my privilege to be his Pastor during that period of his life.

This book is a scholarly presentation of normal experiences in the stages of Christian growth. You will discover each stage to be enlightening, challenging, and clearly presented. I encourage every Christian soldier, and especially every minister of the gospel, to accept Sonny’s invitation to go with him on a journey of each and all of the seasons of his ministry. There is no doubt that you will be profited immensely in your study of his dramatic presentation of the common experiences of Christian growth. I highly recommend this book for every Christian’s library."

Dr. Ken Sumrall, President and Founder
Christian Fellowship Network of Ministers and Churches
Pace, Florida

“I have known Sonny Misar since he came as a student to Liberty Bible College in Pensacola, Florida. It didn’t take me long to see that there was something “special” about this man. I still see that in him. His new book Journey to Authenticity reveals much of the journey on which God has taken this wise pastor. Travel with Sonny in the pages of this book and discover your own area of specialness in Christ."

Pastor Jim Darnell
Bible Conference Speaker
Martindale, Texas

Parry Islands
Baffin's Bay
Hudson's Bay
NORTH
AMERICA
UNITED STATES
Sandwich Isles
Friendly Is
Tierra del Fuego
OCEAN

Journey to Authenticity

Spitsbergen
C T I C
Nova Zembla
Lapland
Archangel
S I B E R I
Petersburg
E U R O P E
R U S S I A
Moscow
A S I A
Aral
TARTARY
Black S.
Arabian Sea
Bengal
I N D I A N
O C E A N
NEW HOLLAND
Pt. Natal
A R C T I C

Journey to Authenticity

Discovering Your Spiritual Identity through the Seasons of Life

R. Sonny Misar

Printed in the United States of America

ISBN: 978-0-979-0296-7-7

Published by MasterPress
318 S. E. 4th Terrace
Cape Coral, FL 33990
1-800-325-9136
www.masterpressbooks.com

Cover and Interior Design/Composition by
Agapé Design Studios, Winona, MN 55987
info@agapedesignstudios.com
©iStockphoto
Author photo by Lisa Howard Photography

Italics or bold within Scripture quotations reflect the author's added emphasis.

Dedication

To my precious mother, Julie, who has been on this incredible journey herself and has helped others find their way so beautifully.

Acknowledgments

Thank you to my amazing wife, Becky, for her support and early draft input on this work and to those who encouraged me to put these thoughts in book form. Much thanks to those who proofed this document and offered helpful insights: Professor Jana Craft, John Larson, Greta Laughlin, Jim Osters and Randy Pierce. Thanks to Jim and Jan Russo for the use of the Florida condo which became a great retreat for writing. Much appreciation goes to Rob and Carol Graham, Rudy and Joann Gast and Andrew and Rosemary Griffo for their extravagant hospitality during my sabbatical. Much appreciation goes to the wonderful leaders and congregation at Living Light Church who gave me time and space to write this book. They have been more than gracious with me as we have traveled these 21 years together. Thanks also to the leadership team of *Ascension Fellowships International* who affirmed my early teachings on the journey. Much appreciation goes to Laurie Nelson at Agapé Design Studios for her outstanding graphic work. Most of all, thank you to our Great Sojourner, the Lord Jesus Christ, who has gone ahead of us on this way.

Table of Contents

Introduction

I invite you to come with me on a journey; a pilgrimage of sorts. This journey is not over land and sea, but is through the passages of the human soul. Our discoveries will not be of gold and lost cities, but of our own identity in Christ. This is a unique journey because it is directed by the hand of God. In fact, the word pilgrimage means a journey to a sacred place. That sacred place is where we find the mysterious mingling of both divine intention and human will. This spiritual journey enables us to discover ourselves, our God and our place in His greater purpose on earth.

The journey of identity development has been the study of great minds, both Christian and secular. The classical Greek philosopher, Socrates, is quoted as wisely saying, *"Know thyself."* Then in 1891, from a more humanistic perspective, Oscar Wilde proclaimed, *"Be thyself."* Finally, Jewish theologian, Abraham Joshua Heschel wrote, *"There is no self-understanding without God-understanding - 'Know thy God' rather than 'Know Thyself' is the categorical imperative of the biblical man."*

Against the backdrop of these seemingly divergent views, we will explore the amazing world of Spiritual Identity Development. Don't let this unwieldy concept put you off. For the ideas of *"Know thyself," "Know thy God"* and *"Be thyself"* actually converge in the process of true spiritual maturity.

You will notice that our journey will take a very practical approach. Much has been written from a theoretical perspective on this topic, but I've designed this book to serve as a personal guide to help travelers understand their own growth process in Christ. It's my prayer that God will use this book to shed light on what can be a mysterious and shadowy road through life. The psalmist said, "Your word is a lamp to my feet and a light for my path." Psalm 119:105

Beyond being another self-help approach, this pilgrimage will allow us to see that **God** is behind our movement and progress. **He** is at the center of this unfolding plan…not us. Indeed, all history is "His story" and we are called to find our place in it.

How is it that we travel and develop in these stages of faith? What does God have to teach us in each of these passages of life? Are there unique dangers for each stage of our pilgrimage? Can my life actually serve God's eternal purpose right here and now? These are some of the questions we will explore as we travel through the life stages of the soul.

Again, I invite you to take this amazing pilgrimage with me. Some of the landscape will feel like home to you and some of it will look quite foreign. One thing I know, we are in for the ride of our lives!

R. Sonny Misar, June, 2010

The Grand Canyon By Night

"Your word is a lamp to my feet
and a light for my path."
— Psalm 119:105

Expectations were high as we began our family vacation and the 1,600 mile trip from Minnesota to Arizona to visit the Grand Canyon. The minivan was packed with more than ample luggage, along with my wife Becky and our four children. While every sight along the way was an enjoyable experience, we were all anticipating the thrill of standing at the rim of the Grand Canyon and gazing over its vast beauty. Seeing this sight for the first time would be the crown jewel of our "out West vacation!"

After a grueling day of travel, the road trip was about to pay off. The problem was that we arrived late at night and found ourselves *directionally disoriented* (guys don't like to use the word "lost"). Now, one of my pet peeves is getting directionally disoriented while driving. To add to that, no one was around to even ask for directions to our motel (another thing guys don't like to do). We were all very tired and ready for this leg of the journey to be done. Our weariness was contrasted by the reality that we were very near this great wonder of the world!

It was one of those pitch black nights when we drove into the Grand Canyon National Park. We were on a two lane stretch of road, seemingly in the middle of nowhere, when I looked to our right. Out the window was an eerie vast darkness; like a night sky without stars. I glanced to our left and saw rest rooms and a parking lot, the usual sights of any park. Then it hit me. Stopping the van right in the middle of the road I said, "Kids, we're here! Look at that! Do you know what that is over there?" I asked, pointing to the right. "You can't see it but it's the Grand Canyon!" We were so close to the rim of the canyon that we could have thrown a stone over the edge, yet it was impossible to see or appreciate because it was shrouded in complete darkness.

Sometimes our life journey is like that. We know we are near something big, but we just cannot see it! We don't have enough light to realize where we are or to understand what is happening to us. It is here that our lives can get "directionally disoriented." This unfortunate state causes us to miss out on seeing all the glories of our immediate life stage. The fact is, our lives are full of seasons – stages of reality and experience that mold who we are.

As you work through this book, you will have the opportunity to visit some of the places you have passed through in life. You will also be invited to go to some places you have yet to experience. There are six distinct phases of growth we will discover on our pilgrimage. I call them the **Stages of Spiritual Identity Development.** With God's help you will be able to gain appreciation for your past, identify where you are presently on the map, and look forward with greater clarity to what lies ahead.

The Importance of Identity

Fellow traveler, God has given us a beautiful promise tied to an incredible pronouncement of our identity in Christ. Proverbs 4:18 says "The path *of the righteous* is like the first gleam of dawn, shining ever brighter till the full light of day." Our identity as children of God is that of "the righteous." This is not a self-righteousness earned by our own religious merit, but a gift from God based on our faith in Christ. God further tells us that He will shed greater and greater light on our path of life. It will be like a glorious sunrise growing from a small sliver of light into the radiance of the noonday sun.

In my years of pastoral ministry I have seen the importance of having a biblical grasp of our identity in Christ. God has spoken some astounding things over us as believers, things so grand that we may have a hard time believing them! Here is something I know to be true: how we see ourselves determines how we live. The fulfillment of our personal destiny in God is linked to how we understand our identity in Him!

A proper grasp of our identity can be tricky business because of the potential ditches on either side of the road. On one side we have the *"I'm no good; I'm a loser"* self-perception. This is how the depressed donkey Eeyore sees himself as he lives with the likes of Christopher Robin and Winnie the Pooh in the Hundred Acre Wood. Just say "hi" to Eeyore and he'll say, *"Thanks for noticing me, but I'm no good anyway."* People with this kind of identity concept expect and attempt very little in life. On the other side are those who have an over-inflated identity concept which leads to pride, permissiveness and arrogance. This person is caught up in a subtle attitude of spiritual entitlement. They think that God works for *them!* They feel that He owes them the "cattle on a thousand hills" and the hills, too! Both of these people have failed to find the sweet center of their true identity in Christ. I believe that this will be the greatest discovery we will make on our journey together. It is the place of **Authenticity** – the place where our true spiritual identity in Christ merges with our very unique and human design. The blend of these two is potent!

So, what does the Bible tell us about our identity? Jesus said, "I no longer call you servants, because a servant does not know his master's business. Instead, **I have called you friends**" (John 15:15). The Apostle Peter affirmed the identity of all believers: "But you are **a chosen people, a royal priesthood, a holy nation, a people belonging to God**..." (1 Peter 2:9a) The Apostle Paul repeatedly underscored the believer's identity in Christ: "God made him who had no sin to be sin for us, **so that in him we might become the righteousness of God.**" (2 Corinthians 5:21) Simply put, God wants us to believe who He says we are. It is not a reward based on our own merit or performance but a gift based on our response to His grace. Here, there is no room for pride or arrogance, but only for grateful hearts saying, "here I am, Lord, send me."

If Satan can get us to believe a lie about who we really are then he can control our lives. He used this weapon (unsuccessfully) on Jesus Christ as he tempted Him in the wilderness. God the Father had just powerfully spoken divine identity over Jesus' life at His baptism when He said for all to hear, "This is my Son, whom I love; with him I am well pleased." Then Jesus was led into the wilderness where He fasted and was tempted by Satan. Two of the three temptations were aimed at confusing and undermining Jesus' true identity. Listen to Satan's subtlety: "The tempter came to him and said, "**If you are the Son of God,** tell these stones to become bread" (Matthew 4:3). And just two verses later: "Then the devil took him to the holy city and had him stand on the highest point of the temple. '**If you are the Son of God,**' he said, 'throw yourself down.'" Just as Satan attempted to undermine Jesus' spiritual identity, he also attempts to deceive us about who we are in Christ.

Further, our spiritual identity concept changes and develops as our journey in life progresses. This is healthy and normal, but there are dangers - we can get stuck. We may stay in one stage too long, trying to recapture our past when we are supposed to be moving on. We can hold so tightly to one identity that we become unwilling to take the next step in God's process of development. Often God will use the painful events that touch our lives as impetus for our movement. This is very easy to read about and much harder to live through. As believers, we may experience a crisis of faith in these confusing seasons. We yell to the heavens, *"God, I have loved you and have given my life to serve You. Why is this happening to me?"* Then we hear the truth of Scripture, "**In all things God works** for the good of those who love him, who have been called according to his purpose. For those God foreknew he also predestined **to be conformed to the likeness of his Son**…" Romans 8:28-29. Through the process of our spiritual identity development, we begin to discover that God is unfolding His divine agenda behind the scenes. Through all our life passages, He is conforming us to the likeness of Christ.

I have laid out the stages of Spiritual Identity Development as a road map. If you are a visual learner like me, this will help you to grasp the dynamics of each stage. Like all road maps, there are designated interstate highways as well as the scenic back roads. For the purpose of clarity, our map will lay out the main interstate route. However, everyone's journey is going to be unique to their life experiences. Don't worry if your personal experience looks a bit different than what I describe on the map. This doesn't mean that you're lost. We are in the same county; you may be just taking a scenic route as you travel that leg of the journey.

Along the way, I will ask you to briefly journal some of your personal reflections. You will find this in each chapter in the sections called *Time to Reflect*. Like looking through an old photo album, some events may come to mind that you have not thought of in many years. You will benefit from the time taken to thoughtfully reflect on these experiences. I also encourage you to pick up this book again in a few years to revisit your movement along the way. Further, your discoveries are best worked into your life if shared in the context of a small group. Great encouragement and insight will be added as you reflect on your journey with some trusted friends.

As we travel together through the stages of Spiritual Identity Development, I pray that the Holy Spirit will be our Travel Guide. God has woven into every life stage a glory all its own. Some of the places, people and experiences of our lives may bring painful memories. This is to be expected, it will afford you the time to see God's hand working through it all, bringing new insights, forgiveness and healing.

That weary night of travel out West eventually led us to our motel where a good night's sleep brought new perspective. In the morning we could not wait to get up and see the majestic sights of the Grand Canyon....this time in the light of day! As we approached the canyon's rim, we breathlessly took in its vast splendor. The Grand Canyon was an amazing sight to behold and well worth the effort it took to get there, but seeing it in the light of day made all the difference! Now, let's get out the map and ask God for light as we get ready to take in some breathtaking views along our journey together.

Now, let's get out the map and ask God for light as we get ready to take in some breathtaking views along our journey together.

"Show me, O LORD, my life's end and the number of my days; let me know how fleeting is my life."

— Psalm 39:4

2

Viewing Life in Stages

"Jesus replied, 'My time has not yet come.' "

—John 2:4

Have you ever heard the expression "the terrible two's" when referring to children? Whether you believe that age to be terrible or terrific, the implication is that there is a stage of life development happening. In the process of raising our children, Becky and I have observed that they pass through developmental stages. Often, when one of the older siblings got frustrated with the behavior of one of their younger siblings, we would explain it by telling them, "Oh, they're going through a stage right now...." While it never took away the frustration of the moment, at least it gave a context to understand such unreasonable behavior...and a hope that no "stage" can last forever!

The idea of movement through life stages is nothing new. Some early church leaders such as Augustine, Aelred of Rievaulx, Julian of Norwich, John of the Cross, Teresa of Avila and Francis of Assisi spoke and wrote of the stages in this journey. In the mid-nineteenth century, Soren Kierkegaard pondered the *Stages on Life's Way.* Recent writers on this important topic include James Fowler and the seven stages of faith, Scott Peck and his four stages on the journey and Janet Hagberg and Robert Guelich in what they describe as the *"Critical Journey."* Robert Hicks uncovers great insight in life stage development in his two books *The Masculine Journey* and *The Feminine Journey.* Dr. J. Robert Clinton has studied Christian leaders in particular and has given us *Leadership Emergence Theory.* While all of these authors offer a unique perspective as they look through the facets of this mysterious diamond, one thing remains consistent: they all see stages in the journey of our soul.

I am deliberately writing this book from an Evangelical Christian viewpoint. Therefore, I will be drawing on Scripture and language from that primary grid of experience. However, as I have studied human progression using the Spiritual Identity Map, I have come to the conclusion that its truths cross the boundaries of culture and even religious or spiritual creed. These insights also translate to the realms of business, marriage and personal development. I have taught the Spiritual Identity Development across denominational lines, across cultural lines in other nations, across generational lines, and to individuals without a religious framework at all. I have discussed it with both theologians and secular psychologists. In each case, they resonated deeply with what they heard. I believe it's because we are all living the human experience. God has a creational design that we are discovering. While studying the process of Spiritual Identity Development will help anyone on their journey, God wants to be intimately involved so that Christ may be more perfectly formed in us. God's principles of life are transcendent. Like the Law of Gravity, they work for everyone. Even if we do not acknowledge Him, His truth will work in the areas to which it is applied.

For many years I have pondered the text in chapter two of John's first epistle where he addresses believers using three different titles: Children, Young Men and Fathers. While this letter is written to all believers, we can also see in it a progression of spiritual maturity. These are not age distinctions or even gender distinctions, but phases in our growth and development as Christians. Note how John describes each and the blessings unique for each stage.

"Children"	"You have known the Father and your sins have been forgiven on account of His name."	Acceptance
"Young Men"	"You are strong and the word of God lives in you; you have overcome the evil one."	Achievement
"Fathers"	"You have known Him Who is from the beginning."	Perspective

One might be tempted to think that the detailed study of our spiritual identity borders on self-absorption and narcissism. However, God is involved here. These are the realms of the inner life where He carries out His hidden and deeper work. If we live with the perspective that all of our life is for God and His glorious purpose, then we should be students of this journey of faith. We can more fully serve God when we are the best we can be at each respective stage of our lives. Moses wisely prayed: "Teach us to number our days aright, that we may gain a heart of wisdom." (Psalm 90:12) When we stand before Christ one day, how we lived out this brief lifespan is all we will have to show. Did we stumble off course? Did we get bogged down in regrets and resentment? Did we get distracted by meaningless sightseeing? Or did we stay on the path marked out for us as we served His purpose on earth? No, in this context, studying the stages of proper life development is not self-serving; it's a matter of God-honoring stewardship!

"The Creator is always the same, but those who are created must pass from a beginning and through a middle course, a growth and progression. And it is for this increase and progress that God has formed them." — Irenaeus (A.H. 4.11)

In Psalm 84:5-7, the Psalmist describes this journey in beautiful, poetic language. "Blessed are those whose strength is in you, who have **set their hearts on pilgrimage.** As they pass through the Valley of Baca (weeping), they make it a place of springs; the autumn rains also cover it with pools. **They go from strength to strength,** till each appears before God in Zion."

Did you notice that our hearts are on a pilgrimage toward Zion, the place of God's presence? This life is more than one experience after another; it is a journey of sorts – an expedition charted by our Heavenly Father. Notice also that this pilgrimage takes us *from strength to strength*. This implies movement. It also implies that God has given us strength for our current stage and that

He will provide a new strength for a future stage. Each stage of our spiritual identity development is crafted by God and appropriate for that time. Like using stepping stones to cross a river, we appreciate the one we are on until it is time to move to the next. God is bringing us through our life journey until we appear before Him in His glorious dwelling - Zion.

Further, the Apostle Paul affirms that this process is initiated, directed and brought to completion by the very hand of God. "I always pray with joy because of your partnership in the gospel from the first day until now, being confident of this, that he who ***began*** a good work in you will **carry it on to completion** until the day of Christ Jesus." Philippians 1:4-6

Living in Minnesota for the last 21 years has afforded us the privilege of enjoying all four distinct seasons. Although, in the dead of winter when the wind is blowing and it's -30 degrees Fahrenheit outside, it's hard to fully appreciate the privilege! I can recall walking outside one such winter, looking at the deadness of the trees, the blowing snow and the frozen lake. In the midst of meditating on my life, God seemed to speak to my heart and say, *"Each season has a glory of its own."* I have taken that to heart through the years of my spiritual journey. While we may see the summer of our soul as glorious, there is a beauty and majesty to our life's winters, too. In these changing seasons we discover both God and ourselves as we never have before. Holding this truth within our hearts allows us to find God's wonder throughout each season of our soul.

As we move into the subsequent chapters we will unfold the road map stage by stage. This will allow us to examine each unique leg of the journey. As with any trip, you may be tempted to rush ahead, skipping sections in order to enjoy others. Just as you can't fast-forward life that way, I encourage you to progress through this adventure and study each life stage in order. Each builds on the other. With this in mind, let's look at a few "travel tips" that will help us understand the stages of our journey.

1. We tend to think that the current stage on our journey will continue to be our experience forever.

I remember my day of awakening while in kindergarten at Henry Winkleman School in Northbrook, Illinois. Our nice teacher was leading us up the stairwell while another teacher was leading her class down. I noticed that this other group was made up of older- looking kids. Curious, I asked a fellow kindergartener, "What are these older kids doing here?" "Oh," he answered with wisdom beyond his years, "these are the first and second graders." "Wait," I mused dumfounded, "you mean to tell me I have to come back next year...and then the year after that? I have to endure more years of this torture following kindergarten graduation?" To this day, I still don't know why that little detail never sunk in for me. Needless to say, what I thought was a nine month boot camp away from mommy turned into a twelve year experience of epic proportions!

Let's face it, we are creatures of habit. We like things to stay the way they are...predictable and according to our expectations. However, our journey through life is not that simple. It changes. Whether we are in an exciting place of fulfillment and peace or a dark place of depression and anguish, this will not be our lot in life forever. Our experience base is all we know and it defines our expectations for the future. Wise King Solomon said, "There is a time for everything, and a season for every activity under heaven. He has made everything beautiful in its time. He has also set eternity in the hearts of men; yet they cannot fathom what God has done from beginning to end" (Ecclesiastes 3:1, 11).

2. We have a "Home Stage" but can visit the other preceding stages in which we've already lived.

As we unfold the Spiritual Identity Map, part of what we will do is identify where we are on our personal journey right now. This is called our Home Stage. Each stage builds on the other; they are cumulative. However, if you are at stage three as a Home Stage, you can move rather freely between stages one, two and three.

"When you're finished changing, you're finished."
— Benjamin Franklin

I have found that younger people tend to place themselves further along on the journey while older people tend to be more objective about their current stage. I remember getting feedback from a group of young Bible college students, excited and growing in their faith. They examined the map and one dogmatically stated, "Oh yeah, I remember when I was there..." as he pointed to a place far beyond his possible experience. I thought to myself, "You *may* have had an experience that looked something like that, my friend, but you haven't yet drunk that goblet down to its dregs!" (Later we will discuss the micro-cyclical nature of our spiritual identity development.)

God is faithful to walk with us through the uniqueness of each of our life stages. As we allow Him to work in us, we are able to turn back to help others through the stages we have lived. The Apostle Paul said it this way, "Praise be to God...who comforts us in all our troubles, so that we can comfort those in any trouble with the comfort we ourselves have received from God." 2 Corinthians 1:3-4

3. One stage is not better or more spiritual than any of the others; each has their appropriate place.

We must be very clear on this point. When we see graduating numbers and more time elapsing in the advanced levels, we can misunderstand the later stages as the better stages. This is not the case.

Each life stage is appropriate for its own time. I would not throw the car keys to a six-year-old and say, "Go out driving with your friends and have a good time." However, let about ten years pass along with the appropriate training and it would be perfectly appropriate, albeit just a little nerve-wracking! After all, teenagers should act like teenagers, not old men! I love their energy, carefree manner and "yes, I CAN conquer the world" attitude! Similarly, I love sitting with those who have lived long and fruitful lives and listening to the wisdom in their stories. They are the often 'overlooked sages' of our time. Ironically, too often the young are striving to be older and the older yearn to recapture their youth. However, great peace comes when we can spiritually 'find our feet' and embrace our current life stage for all it is.

The fact is, we tend to look down on others in earlier stages and misunderstand those in future stages. When I was in my mid-twenties and recently graduated from Bible college, I accepted my first full-time ministry position as a youth pastor at a church in southern Illinois. Yes, I had the answers, with an abundance of zeal and anointing to match. I was locked and loaded, ready for any ministry situation - I was bulletproof for Jesus! My sister Sally and brother-in-law Fred attended the same church with their family. Fred was ten years older than I was and had experienced plenty of life and ministry... with scars to prove it. Fred was a Christian family man, a truck tire builder, a realist. In many of life's arena's he had "been there and done that." When bulletproof Sonny came on the scene, ready to extinguish hell with a squirt gun, Fred had one thing to say to me: *"Sonny, you are young and idealistic."* Not to be squelched, I shot back, "Fred, you are old and cynical!" To me Fred was a burnt-out believer sitting on the sidelines while eternity's most exciting game was going on right under his nose. "Fred," I chided him, "I'd rather aim for something and miss it than to aim for nothing and *hit it!"* What I didn't know was that spiritually and emotionally, Fred didn't need my simple fixes. He needed someone to hear him, understand him and bandage his wounds with compassion. The lesson here is that both Fred and I were on the same journey. We were just at different places on the map.

Suppose you had four guests visiting the United States of America from a remote African village. They had never been outside of their village, but you gave them each a car, placed them in four different parts of the U.S.A. and told them to explore and report back as to what this country was like. The one you dropped in New York City would confidently say that the U.S. was full of tall buildings, much traffic and crowds of people. The one you placed in the upper Midwest would report that this country was a vast, flat farmland with corn, wheat and soybean fields as far as the eye could see. The African visitor placed in the Rocky Mountains would declare that this great nation is rugged, wooded and full of great mountains. The final guest you placed in California might say that there was a vast ocean on one side with cities, vineyards and many unusual people walking around! Which of your guests would be right? They *all* would be! Each was speaking out of their own perspective, their own experience. One of the great benefits of understanding the stages of spiritual identity is the ability to relate with understanding and compassion to those ahead of you and behind you in this great journey.

Now we are ready to further unfold this map and to journey to places both known and unknown. With humility comes wisdom, so let's proceed with a strong dependence on God for His guidance. Speeding on these roads is not advised. Take time to appreciate your surroundings.

Buckle up. Let's go!

3

When the Light Comes On

Stage One: "New Life"

"Therefore, if anyone is in Christ,
he is a new creation; the old has gone,
the new has come!"

— 2 Corinthians 5:17

"My friend, Jamie, invited me to go to a Christian concert. The music was great, but what really impacted me was the message of the band. They spoke of knowing Jesus in such a close way. When they talked about how we need to ask Jesus to forgive us of our sins, I knew they were talking about me. I walked to the front after the concert and prayed with one of the counselors. My life has totally changed and now I am telling others about what Jesus can do!"

"Last Easter at church it all became real to me. When I heard the pastor talk about what Jesus did on the cross, I was deeply moved. He challenged us to go beyond knowing about Jesus to receiving Him. I prayed the prayer at the end of the service and I felt a weight lift from my life. It's hard to explain, but for the first time I feel clean before God. I thank God for what Jesus did for me on the cross!"

"I had successfully devastated my life with drug abuse. It was only through my treatment that I began to think that there might be a God who was loving and personal. God found me (or I found God) in the most desperate time in my life. My sponsor has been a big help in leading me to Jesus."

"I was raised in a church-going family. As a teenager, my parents made me attend church, but it never meant that much to me. When I was 20 years old, they couldn't force me to go anymore so I just slept in every Sunday. God was totally not in the picture through my college and young adult life. But after the birth of my son, I began to think about all the evil in the world and how he needed some Christian upbringing. My husband and I began attending a great church near our home. While we initially went for our son, we now go for ourselves. I have been experiencing God as I never had before. I look forward to growing in Christ as a family."

Spiritual Identity Map

Ideal Self

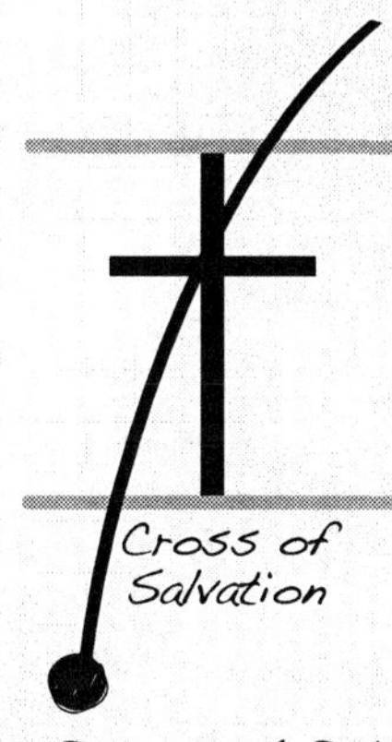

Despised Self

We begin our journey with an amazing experience.

It is the event of our personal salvation. It is that moment we realize we are desperately lost and in need of a Savior. Up to that point we were living in what I call our "Despised Self." This was a place of spiritual darkness, sin and despair. For many of us, our lives in this realm were filled with actions, attitudes and addictions that held us down. However, as the map shows, we begin our journey when we are lifted out of the miry clay of Despised Self and brought to the foot of the cross of Christ. Here, we are humble and needy; we understand that we cannot save ourselves. We need Jesus. In the words of that great hymn sung at Billy Graham crusades around the world, *"Just as I am without one plea, but that Thy blood was shed for me. And that Thou biddest me come to Thee, O Lamb of God I come. I come."*

"Yet to all who received him, to those who believed in his name, he gave the right to become children of God.
—John 1:12

It is here that our knowledge about God shifts into an experience with God. This might happen while we are at a Bible study or at a church service. It could come about while talking with a friend about spiritual things or being alone in a quiet place. Regardless of our surroundings, we are believing, receiving and supernaturally becoming a child of God! This is our spiritual awakening; this is when the lights come on!

What brought you to this place of new life? Was there a crisis, a loss or an awareness of your need? Did you come to Christ on your own? Was there a friend or a minister speaking to you? Did someone share a Bible verse with you? Were you listening to a preacher on the TV or radio? Did your salvation happen in a moment or was it progressive and over time? Perhaps you wept, perhaps you rejoiced with great joy; maybe you didn't feel much of anything. Were you raised always "knowing about God" or did Christ save you out of a place of deep bondage? It is very important to revisit our personal experience of salvation in Christ. This was the launching place of our New Life!

Whether this was a vivid and memorable experience or not, the fact remains that there was a spiritual awakening that occurred in your life and you came alive on the inside. Jesus calls this being "born again" (John 3:3). You went from being bound for hell to being bound for heaven. The Bible says that "there is rejoicing in the presence of the angels of God over one sinner who repents" (Luke 15:10).

The cross was the cruelest implement of torture and death invented by mankind, yet this old rugged cross became the final sacrificial altar to remove sin from the human soul. It was here that final atonement was made. Upon the cross, the righteous wrath of God against our sinful rebellion was satisfied. Through Christ's work on the cross, God now imparts His righteousness to us. Once we were enemies of God, now we are beloved children in His family. Christ, the perfect sacrificial Lamb, paid what we could never pay. His shed blood covered our sin once and for all.

> "Therefore, there is now **no condemnation** for those who are in Christ Jesus, because through Christ Jesus the law of the Spirit of life set me free from the law of sin and death."
> —Romans 8:1-2

For the first time, we begin to understand the lightness of soul that comes from being brought out of spiritual condemnation. We leave our "Despised Self" behind as if it was a rotting corpse and launch into a place we never thought possible. Entering the realm of the "Ideal Self" we feel like soaring eagles. There are new things to see and understand. The Bible suddenly makes sense to us as the Holy Spirit opens up truth from its pages. Prayer flows out of us like breathing. God is our Father now and wants to hear all our concerns, questions and praises. Awe and wonder now fill our lives. There is purpose and meaning to life as we begin to see ourselves in God's plan. We can say, with the man that Jesus healed after being blind from birth, "One thing I do know. I was blind but now I see" (John 9:25)!

My "New Life" Story...

My mom bent over to look into my five year old face. She answered my questions about going to heaven and being forgiven of my sin. There was no pressure or coercion in her approach. In my young heart, I knew that I was a sinner in need of forgiveness. My mother quoted Jesus' words in Revelation 3:20 "Here I am! I stand at the door and knock. If anyone hears my voice and opens the door, I will come in and eat with him, and he with me." I knew that I had to open the door of my heart to Him. The Holy Spirit was powerfully drawing me to Jesus. In my conviction, I ran out of her room, down the hall and into my bedroom. Then I got in my closet, closing the door behind me. There, alone, I knelt and prayed a very simple prayer asking Jesus to forgive me of my sin and to come into my heart. In that moment, a glory descended on my young life and filled me with a supernatural joy and rapture! I was so excited that I ran out of my closet, out of my room and down the hallway. There I knocked on my parents' door exclaiming, "Mom, I did it! I did it!" Opening the door she asked, "What did you do, Sonny?" "You know, I did it!" I said. Wanting me to give words of confession to this spiritual experience she asked again, "What did you do?" "I received Jesus into my heart!" I proclaimed with joy overflowing.

NO.

DATE

Time to Reflect...

Take a moment of reflection right now and revisit that time or season in your life. Don't be in a hurry. You may want to close your eyes. Go ahead and relive this turning point in your life.

Where were you?

Who spoke to you about Christ?

What key truths do you remember being shared with you?

Did you feel anything as you received Christ? If so, what?

Trouble in Paradise

With every developmental stage there are areas of weakness and pitfalls to avoid. As the evangelist once said about moving on with God, "New levels, new devils!" Let's look at just a few of these obstacles. After our initial sense of cleansing and forgiveness, we discover (usually sooner than later) that we still have a sinful nature which needs to come under the control of the Spirit. Our sins can leave us feeling overcome with a sense of unworthiness. The Stage One believer must understand that our SIN was removed at the cross, but that a Christian will still have to deal with their propensity to commit SINS. The first deals with our legal standing before God; our SIN was completely removed and we were given Christ's righteousness. The second (SINS) are those individual acts of omission or commission that are outside of God's will. Dealing with SINS is the ongoing process called progressive sanctification. This involves our cooperation with the Holy Spirit to make us more Christ-like in action and attitude. Scripture tells us what to do as Christians who sometimes sin. 1 John 1:9 says that "If we confess our sins, he is faithful and just and will forgive us our sins and purify us from all unrighteousness." New believers are sometimes afraid that they will wear out 1 John 1:9, but that's impossible. Every sincere prayer of repentance and renunciation is heard and answered by our merciful God. However, Christ's commitment to ongoing forgiveness must never be used as a license for living in sin. When you came to Christ, God gave you "amazing grace" not "greasy grace"(a sloppy grace that lets our sins just slide by). Grace is not only God's unmerited favor, but also the power of God to do the will of God. That same grace will lead you to walk away from sinful life choices.

"For the grace of God that brings salvation has appeared to all men. It teaches us to say "No" to ungodliness and worldly passions, and to live self controlled, upright and godly lives in this present age."

—Titus 2:11-13

Unfortunately, many Christians have allowed strongholds to remain in their lives, making them slaves to a particular sin. (A stronghold is a fortress of thought built on a lie.) They are born-again children of God who walk in continual defeat because they cannot fully leave certain elements of their old life. A good Christian counselor or pastor can be a great help in walking us through steps to freedom by exposing the lie at the root of these strongholds.

Another weakness for the Stage One believer is having an over-dependence on feelings as they relate to Christ. If we suddenly don't feel as close to God as we once did, it may seem we have fallen out of grace or lost our salvation. However, walking in spiritual confidence is like a train. FAITH is the engine leading the way, pulling the car of FACTS and the caboose of FEELINGS behind. When we get these three cars out of order, our train is bound to crash. FACT and FEELING are part of our train, but the Christian life is a life led firmly by the engine of FAITH! Christians must maintain this order if they are to walk in victory.

"You, dear children, are from God and have **overcome** them,
because the one who is in you is greater
than the one who is in the world." —1 John 4:4

Individuals in Stage One of their Spiritual Identity Development can also be hindered because they have not yet learned God's Word and His ways. Storms of life will come to a new believer and can throw them into despair and confusion. The trial may be adverse circumstances, wrongs we've committed or wrongs committed against us. It may be a rejection by friends or any number of difficulties in life. These adversities can be devastating for the young in faith because they have not been rooted in God's Word. God wants us to know more than just his deeds of power; He wants us to know His ways. Psalm 103:7 says that "He made known his **ways** to Moses, his **deeds** to the people of Israel." The Psalmist proclaims, "I have hidden your word in my heart that I might not sin against you (Psalm 119:11). Jesus was able to answer and overcome Satan's temptations as He countered each one with the Word of God, saying, "It is written..." (Matthew 4:4,7,10).

Knowing some of the potential sticking points of Stage One can keep us from getting derailed in our journey of faith. Satan and his minions are very real foes. They are not happy when we become part of God's family and will do all they can to deceive and discourage us. Thank God, we have His Word and His Spirit!

It's Only the Beginning!

For each developmental stage I will offer some guidance for moving on. Spiritual development is a mysterious blend of divine invitation and human response. These transitions often go unnoticed by us and can take years to fully pass through. God is the orchestrator of each of these transitions through our life journey. As mentioned earlier, He can use many circumstances to usher us into a new stage. Some of God's tools of movement can look like a crisis of some kind, a deep sense of need, an unrelenting dissatisfaction, a personal tragedy, a relational difficulty or an awakening to a new perspective. We may move at the prodding of a job transition, a spiritual revelation, a physical illness or a strong challenge from a coach, pastor or mentor, to name a few.

While we cannot speed up our progress, I believe we can delay our transitions. Like kids in the back seat during a long road trip, we call out to God, *"Are we there yet?"* In some of our more painful seasons we may want to hit the fast forward button and skip to the next chapter, but we can't. God is involved as He works with our soul. The process of God unfolding His will in our lives looks like two ballroom dancers on the dance floor. One leads, the other must follow. In this example a timeless principle is demonstrated: divine initiation must be followed by human response. This principle is how Noah built the ark and how Christ went to the cross - divine initiation, human response. It was the pattern of how we entered our new life in Christ and is the way we progress as a mature disciple - divine initiation, human response. We must keep this in mind as we consider our passage through all the stages of Spiritual Identity Development.

"It is good to be between a ruined house of bondage and a holy promised land." — Leonard Cohen

So what are some of the things we can do to cooperate with God as He moves us from Stage One to Stage Two? The input of strong, supportive relationships is vital to our movement from Stage One to Stage Two. Perhaps we experienced the tearing away of some unhealthy relationships when we lived in the realm of the Despised Self. It is powerful when a new believer impacts the lives of their unsaved friends, but one should also be wise to discern who is making the greater impact. At times, painful departures are necessary. Supportive relationships lead us toward growth in Christ and encourage loving obedience to Christ's commands. Our best allies can be those living in Stage Two or Three. They spur us on by example to the kind of life we crave. Often they have come to know the Word and ways of God more deeply. Their counsel and input can save us from getting sidetracked and stuck in Stage One.

Taking in the Word of God and fellowship are also imperative for progress. They are like high-octane fuel for our car as we travel down the road of identity development. I remember having a new, deep desire to read my Bible and to journal my findings at this transition in my life. I looked forward to youth meetings. I could not get enough of church services and small group Bible studies. What was happening here? Remember, Psalm 84:7, "They go from strength to strength, till each appears before God in Zion." God was bringing me from the strength of Stage One to the strength of Stage Two.

There are battles to be fought and won at this level. The patterns of our Despised Self are in our rear view mirror, but still not that far away. Believers in Stage One must be challenged to leave those old ways, thought patterns and habits and to move on in God. We cannot run the race marked out for us if we are dragging along the baggage of our past life (Hebrews 12:1).

"You were taught, with regard to your former way of life,
to **put off** your old self, which is being corrupted by its deceitful desires;
to be made new in the attitude of your minds;
and to **put on** the new self, created to be like God
in true righteousness and holiness."
— Ephesians 4:22-24

My mid-teen years were focused on playing guitar in a rock-and-roll band. I gave my time to practicing, learning new licks and jamming with our band. My ambition in life was to be discovered and make it big. Little did I know that I was competing with about half of the youth population of the western civilized world at that time! Enter Randy Pierce, our new youth pastor. He came into our youth group with a clarion call for righteous living, sharing our faith and serving God's purpose. This was no *"entertain the kids and make them happy"* approach to youth ministry. Pastor Randy put the bar high and challenged us to rise to it. We did.

One day he confronted me on the place of music in my life. He said, "Sonny, you know that Jesus said in Matthew 12:30 that if you are not *for* Him you're *against* Him. And if you are not gathering with Him you are scattering....Is your music for Jesus or against Him?" (Pastor Randy had a way of being lovingly direct.) Aided by the working of the Holy Spirit, that challenge got me moving forward, resulting in the decision to dedicate my musical talents to the work of the Lord. This was pivotal in my spiritual movement at that time. I had to break free of some old life patterns that were near and dear to me. A putting down of something precedes every passage. As Dr. John Maxwell says, "You've got to give up to go up."

Celebrate Grace

If you find yourself at Stage One, I encourage you to celebrate the grace of God that has been extended to you. Realize that His grace has brought you into a new relationship with Jesus Christ. Like any relationship, it must be fostered if it is going to grow. Let prayer flow from you like you were talking with a good friend. Allow the Holy Spirit to speak to you as you read the Bible. Learn to obey God's promptings even in the little things. Begin to build friendships with other strong believers and worship regularly in a life-giving church. Tell others about what God has done in your life and encourage them to come to Christ for salvation.

Remember, God's grace was a gift to you. It is not only the power to save you from sin, it is also that which will carry you into maturity as a believer. While God wants your obedience, there is nothing you can do to earn His ongoing favor. Continue to exercise your faith and trust in Him for every step forward. Celebrate the power of His grace which helps you say "no" to sin, wrong attitudes and bad habits.

The spiritual awakening of Stage One has introduced us to a whole new life purpose and destiny. There is a glorious horizon ahead just waiting to be explored! These are exciting times of growth and discovery. The heavenly payoffs are far more valuable than anything we are asked to leave behind. Stage Two is right around the corner and what an exciting place of growth it is! I hope you have your hiking shoes on because it looks like we're going to do some climbing! I look forward to traveling there with you.

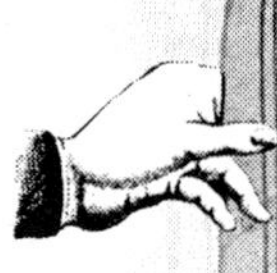

Going the Second Mile

Read Luke 5:1-11 and note the elements of Simon Peter's salvation account. Which of these elements did you experience when you stepped into New Life?

Internet search the song "Who Am I?" by Casting Crowns and listen to the song and consider your new identity in Christ.

Meditate on the beautiful artwork of Thomas Blackshear in "Forgiven" portraying the wonder of salvation at www.blackshearonline.com

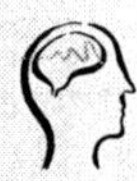

Memorize a great Stage One verse of Scripture in I Peter 2:1-3.

Find an old hymnal or Internet search the classic hymns: "At Calvary" by William R. Newell and "What a Friend we Have in Jesus" by Joseph M. Scriven and meditate on how they paint your spiritual picture.

Stage 1 – "New Life" Highlights

Strengths:

- *The love of God your Father*
- *Freedom and Forgiveness*
- *Awe and wonder of God's goodness*
- *Purpose and Meaning*

Weaknesses:

- *Sense of unworthiness*
- *Over-dependence on feelings*
- *Ignorance of God's Word and ways*
- *Not fully leaving our old life*

Moving On:

- *Build Supportive Relationships*
- *Take in the Word and fellowship*
- *Break patterns of your old life*

Life Stage Axiom:

- *Celebrate Grace*

Notes

Growing in Knowledge and Experience

Stage Two: "Learner"

"Like newborn babies,
crave pure spiritual milk, so that by it
you may grow up in your salvation, now that
you have tasted that the Lord is good."

— 1 Peter 2:2-3

"I still consider myself a relatively new believer. Lately, I have been devouring the Bible, reading as many as five chapters a day. I have so many questions and I am finding them answered in scripture. Every time I pick up my Bible, it feels like I'm eating a healthy meal."

"The guys in my small group really help me stay accountable. We are free to talk about any struggles we may be having. As we go through the book study, I am learning how to be a man of God. I have shared things with these guys that I thought I'd never share with anyone else. We have really gotten to know one another and challenge each other in our areas of weakness."

"Our pastor gives great messages every Sunday. I am learning things that I can actually apply to my life. In the church I was raised in all I remember hearing were irrelevant messages. At F.C.C. my faith has really taken off. Pastor Ken has a grasp of the biblical languages and church history. Listening to him is like sitting in a Bible college class! Now I look forward to church every Sunday."

"God seems to be leading me from one lesson to the next. One month He seems to teach me about faith then the next He emphasizes obedience and then loving others. It seems that He sets up opportunities for me to be stretched in each of the lessons I'm learning. It's like having my own personal life coach."

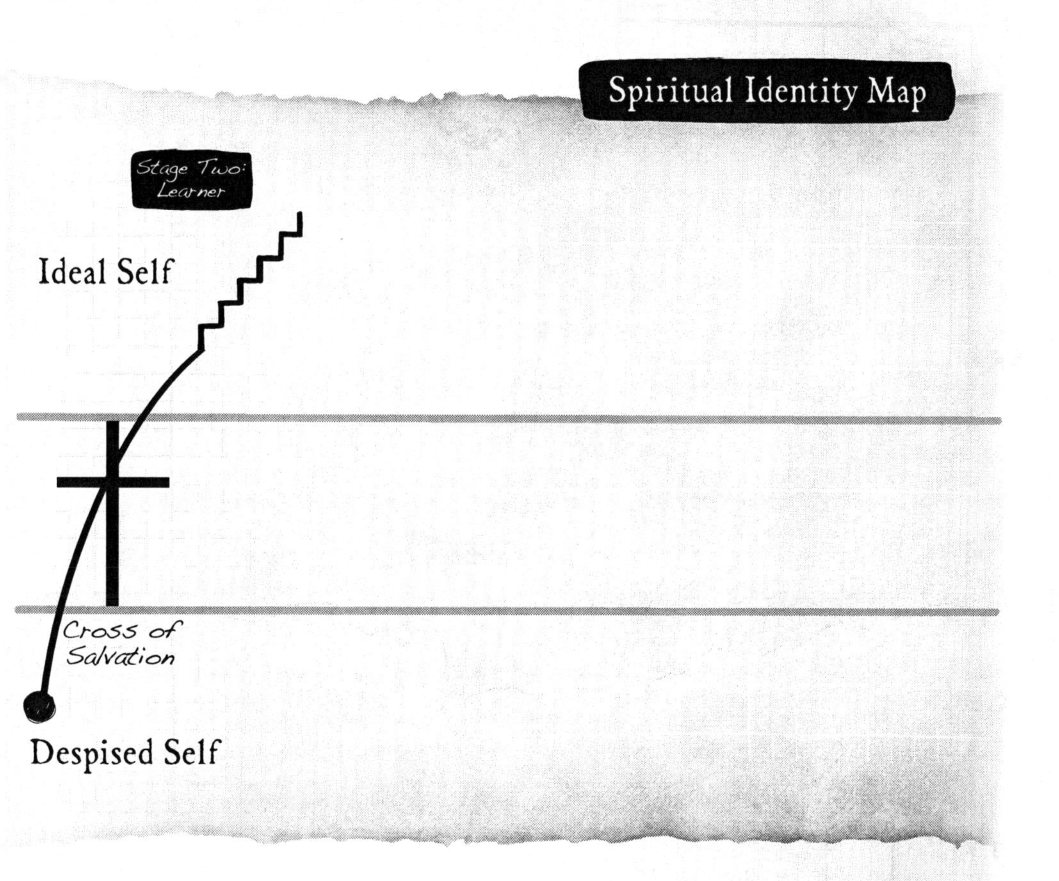

As you study the Spiritual Identity Map above, notice that Stage Two has us progressing higher into the new and exciting realm of Ideal Self. This "Learner" stage will take us to heights we never dreamed possible. Here we are like dry sponges drinking in everything we can. We have a hunger for knowing the Word of God. We delight in how practically it can be applied to our life. We begin anticipating God's guidance in our everyday circumstances.

Notice that the map shows this stage as stair-steps. The vertical rise represents the learning of a particular truth. The horizontal run represents the actual application of that truth to our lives. This is a vital two-step progression for authentic spiritual growth: understanding God's Word (vertical) and then obeying that Word (horizontal). The Apostle James, the Lord's brother (or more accurately, his half brother), spoke of how important it is for these two to work together in our lives.

"Do not **merely listen to the word,** and so deceive yourselves. **Do what it says.** Anyone who listens to the word but does not do what it says is like a man who looks at his face in a mirror and, after looking at himself, goes away and immediately forgets what he looks like. But the man who looks intently into the perfect law that gives freedom, and continues to do this, not forgetting what he has heard, but doing it-he will be blessed in what he does."
—James 1:22-25

God faithfully and patiently works with us at this level by providing new understanding, followed by a test or life situation in which to apply that truth. This is a very significant time in our spiritual development. Vital foundation stones are laid in our lives at this time as God takes us from one lesson to another. These "steps of learning" are lessons given to us by our teachers as well as wisdom directly taught to us by the dealings of God. Sadly, people who have not applied themselves to this kind of inner development often have gaps in their character which show up in future stages. The importance of progressing up the stair steps of learning and applying truth cannot be overstated.

In Stage One, New Life, we were filled with the wonder of God's gift of salvation. We were caught up in the love God has for us and filled with a deep sense of gratitude and awe. Now, as a Stage Two Learner we begin to add knowledge to that wonder. Our sense of ignorance is being replaced with a deeper understanding of God's Word and ways. We grow in confidence as some of our questions are being answered with biblical truth.

One of the powerful things we begin to discover in Stage Two is who we really are in Christ. In Stage One we were happy to sing, "Jesus loves me this I know; for the Bible tells me so." Now God begins to show us not only that He loves us, but all that He has given us in His Son! We begin adding to our faith, goodness and to our goodness, knowledge… (II Peter 1:5). A deeper grasp of our identity in Christ gives us new confidence and authority. It informs us of our spiritual rights and privileges as "kids of the King." Here we begin to explore the glorious implications that came with our new birth in Christ.

In the 1970's there was a poster that was very popular with Christians. It could be found hanging in bedrooms, Sunday school classrooms, dorm rooms or studies. In the center of the poster were the large words, "Who I am In Christ" and surrounding it in rainbow colors were all the many biblical affirmations defining who we are as children of God. There is something potent about being reminded of our "birthright" in God's family!

"Nobody ever outgrows Scripture; the Book widens and deepens with our years."
— Charles H. Spurgeon

At Stage Two we also develop a strong connection to the body of Christ. Those who are growing with us in this flourishing season become our family. Indeed, they spiritually are a part of the family of God. We develop a deep love for those with us on this journey. Our common commitments, beliefs and values weld our hearts together. Perhaps for the first time in our lives, we experience what the Bible calls in the original Greek, "koinonia" – that common sharing, community and fellowship with those of our spiritual family.

"And they continued steadfastly in the apostles' doctrine and fellowship ("koinonia"), and in breaking of bread, and in prayers."
— Acts 2:42

During this season, our teachers and mentors become like spiritual fathers and mothers. We are eager apprentices who find comfort in belonging to something much larger than ourselves. Because there is so much to learn, we can find ourselves unsure and insecure as we launch into Stage Two. We feel like neophytes in this vast expanse of truth and spiritual life. Often, a Stage Two Learner will attach himself/herself to an electrifying leader or strong teacher for needed guidance. This can be of great help to us as we seek to grow, but, taken out of balance, can also be the stuff of codependent and cultic devotion. An example of this can be seen in the university classroom where students who are hungry to believe in *everything* their professor says without considering other perspectives. In a healthy context, however, Stage Two is a season of acquiring knowledge and being challenged to apply it to our lives.

Personally, I was never a great student in my grade school years. I was happy to get C's and an occasional D as long as I graduated on to the next grade. However, something dramatically shifted in my life in the middle of high school. God ushered me into the Stage Two and my spiritual development began skyrocketing. What is interesting is that this stage also impacted my academic achievements. By my senior year I was exceeding students who once were far above me. I remember one class in particular in which I got an A, and another much brighter classmate got a B. For me it was a defining moment! I was beginning to see myself as a Learner, a person of greater potential. Upon entering college I knew that I would be challenged with a whole new dimension of academic rigor. I remember specifically praying an audacious prayer at the beginning of my freshman year: "God," I said, promising to study hard and do my best, "would you help me get straight A's this semester?" God answered that prayer! I continued to pray it at the beginning of each subsequent semester. To His glory, this former C and D student was able to graduate college with a perfect GPA.

Time to Reflect...

NO.

DATE

As you look at the stair-steps of Stage Two, think about some of the big lessons you've learned.

What was one of your major lessons learned in this stage?

How did you apply that to your life?

NO.

DATE

Using one or two words, write on the stairs below. Remember, the vertical line represents the lesson you learned and the horizontal line is how you applied that to your life.

Knowledge Puffs Up...

I Corinthians 8:1 gives us insight into one of the potential weaknesses of the Learner Stage. It says, "Knowledge puffs up, but love builds up." As we grow in our knowledge base, we can take up strong dogmas resulting in critical attitudes and judgmental words. After all, when you know the deeper truths of faith and see other people not following suit, they need to be told...right?! At this stage we can be like Deputy Barney Fife from the great TV series, *The Andy Griffith Show.* We have a gun and we're not afraid to use it, but we only have been entrusted with one bullet. More often than not, however, we see Barney accidentally discharging his one bullet into the floor (which is why Andy requires him to keep it in his pocket)!

In Stage Two we can also fall prey to the "us against them" mentality. Having discovered our standing in truth we tend to draw lines of acceptance around those in "our camp." We are quite comfortable living in our personal realm of conviction; it gives us a sense of identity and security. Those of different viewpoints must be relegated to the category of "off base." It is very seductive at Stage Two to believe that what is "right in our eyes" should be right for everyone else. I am not painting biblical mandates as negotiable, but rather addressing those nondescript issues the Apostle Paul refers to as "disputable matters." (Romans 14:1) Often what we deem right in our personal conviction is not even on the radar screen for another Jesus-loving person. The goal of healthy development is to grow in knowledge *and* wisdom, conviction *and* love. As wise christian leaders have said throughout church history, "In necessary things, unity; in doubtful things, liberty; in all things, charity."

I was in my junior year of Bible college when I returned to suburban Chicago to live at home and work for the summer. It was a great time of personal growth for me. I was definitely enjoying the exhilaration of being a Stage Two Learner. My studies had given me deeper insight in the Word of God and some of my travels had broadened my experience base. I remember attending a worship service at our home church with my family. This was the very church God had used to deeply impact my life just a few years earlier. As I sat in the pew taking in the service, my critical mind was preoccupied with everything that was WRONG with the church's ministries. Why were they praising with such little passion? Why was the preacher preaching such shallow messages? Why was the general spiritual climate so cold? Dear Lord, could it be that our church had turned into the church of Laodicea while I was away (Revelation 3:14-21)? However, what was going on in my heart had more to do with MY issues than the perceived shortcomings of my home church. It is a truly unique person who can go through Stage Two and avoid this kind of judgmental undertone. One of the weaknesses of this stage is the misconception that knowing a truth automatically makes it part of you.

Some people, in their search for pure and undiluted truth, find it hard to put up with their "dead" church. In determined zeal, they set out to find (or establish) their own group. While I believe there are times this can be appropriate, too often it is fueled by limited grace and loss of mature perspective. It is an amusing study (although unfortunate) to observe churches that have split away from their original group because of a disagreement in doctrine or practice. Note what they name their new church group. If they broke away from spiritual legalism they may name their new church "Grace Tabernacle" or something similar. If they separated based on the fact that their old church was not flowing in the Spirit, the new church may be called, "Spirit of Life Center." Those who left because they were looking for real doctrinal purity may call themselves "Berean Bible Church." The pendulum swings in church life, doesn't it? Church history, both ancient and recent, bears the scars of cold love coupled with overheated dogma.

"It is good to grasp the one and not let go of the other.
The man who fears God will avoid all extremes."
— Ecclesiastes 7:18

Moving from Theoretical to Practical

Healthy growth in Stage Two will begin to propel us into our next stage of Spiritual Identity Development. We have learned much and gained a greater sense of confidence. We step out and begin to seek responsibilities in serving and leadership. Perhaps a mentor invites us to help teach a class or lead a devotional on a retreat. Having discovered our God-given gifts, we begin to venture out and actually put them to use. This time can be filled with great exhilaration and terror, but if we continue to make ourselves available, God rewards us with new horizons of spiritual growth. We begin to learn the timeless principle of Matthew 25:21 "Well done, good and faithful servant! You have been faithful with a few things; I will put you in charge of many things."

I served as a resident assistant for two years during my time at Bible college. I was living in the dorm with a group of other young men who, like myself, were training for ministry. Many of us had hopes, dreams and aspirations of doing great things for God. One of my responsibilities was to make sure that the "dorm duties" were completed by these "men of God." The rotating cleaning schedule included such tasks as scrubbing toilets, mopping floors, vacuuming the halls, dusting, and cleaning the mirrors. To my dismay, I had a terrible time getting many of these anointed future leaders to do these menial tasks. Sadly, some of the most gifted were the worst offenders. It became a leadership mantra among us, *"If you are faithful in the little things, God will reward you with more!"* Thankfully, many passed the test and went on to do great things for God.

Another important step forward into Stage Three is the discovery of our distinct, God-given gifts. We may take a spiritual gifts survey and find the unique way in which God has wired us to serve Him. Romans 12:6-8 is often a place we go to discover our "Motivational Gifts." We find a sense of confirmation as we pour over the seven specific gifts and discover that one or two of them fit us like a glove.

"We have different gifts, according to the grace given us. If a man's gift is prophesying, let him use it in proportion to his faith. If it is serving, let him serve; if it is teaching, let him teach; if it is encouraging, let him encourage; if it is contributing to the needs of others, let him give generously; if it is leadership, let him govern diligently; if it is showing mercy, let him do it cheerfully."
— Romans 12: 6-8

This opens up a whole new dimension to our spiritual lives. Suddenly we begin to see ourselves not only as receivers, but contributors as well. We set out to develop and use our gifts in various aspects in and outside of the church. We begin to exercise spiritual authority both in our realm of serving others and in prayer. Part of our learning comes from the realization that we are in a spiritual battle with our three enemies: the world, the flesh and the devil. The taste of victory in these areas is sweet. The sword of the Spirit is the Word of God, which we have learned to pick up and wield in the face of God's enemies (Ephesians 6:17), God is actually using US to advance His Kingdom! What could be better?

Learn All You Can

If you are a Stage Two learner, my advice to you is to learn all that you can. God has much for you to discover about his Word and ways. Grow in both knowledge and wisdom. Let this knowledge reveal God's will to you and wisdom reveal His ways to you. Pour over the Word of God and apply it to your everyday life. Begin to serve others in love, based on the unique ways that God has gifted you. Sit under the teachings of sound and solid Bible instructors. Take new steps of faith based on what you are learning of God's Word and His ways. Stretch yourself by offering to serve in areas of ministry that draw on your unique gifting.

Well, fellow traveler, there are some exciting days ahead! You'd better hang on because some of the highest highs of our journey are just around the corner. Let's unfold the map a bit more and discover the next stretch of road. It looks like it has some twists and turns, mountains and valleys. This will be quite a ride! Put the pedal to the metal, let's go!

Going the Second Mile

II Timothy 2:15 says, "Do your best to present yourself to God as one approved, a workman who does not need to be ashamed and who correctly handles the word of truth." Consider this question: What does it mean for you to handle the truth correctly in your own life?

Write the name of a former (or current) mentor, teacher or leader here. ____________________ Contact them and share with them how they have impacted your life.

Consider an important passage for all Stage Two Learners: Hebrews 5:11–6:2.

Discover your "Motivational Gifts" by taking the free on line assessment at: www.mintools.com and list your top three gifts:
1) ____________________ 2) ____________________
3) ____________________

Internet search the lyrics to the great hymn "In the Garden" by Austin Miles. Consider how it describes your relationship with Christ.

Stage 2 – "Learner" Highlights

Strengths:

- Discovery of your identity in Christ
- Hunger for the Word of God
- Deep love for the family of God

Weaknesses:

- Judgmental of others
- "Us against them" mentality
- Knowledge without wisdom

Moving On:

- Identify your unique gifts in God
- Seek responsibility in serving
- Begin to exercise spiritual authority

Life Stage Axiom:

- "Learn All You Can"

Notes

Fighting for What's Right

Stage Three: "Warrior"

"I write to you, young men,
because you are strong,
and the word of God lives in you,
and you have overcome the evil one."

— 1 John 2:14

"My pastor must see something in me. I never would have thought that I could lead the choir at church. He literally had to talk me into accepting this position, now I can see how God is working through me. People have said that last year's Christmas concert was the best yet. I never thought of myself as a leader, but I guess that is one of the gifts God has given me. All the glory goes to God for using me in this way. I want to continue to use my gifts for His purpose.

"Since I've been baptized in the Holy Spirit my life has a new power. Before, I used to be afraid to witness for Christ. Now I have a new boldness. God has used me to speak into other people's lives with real clarity. I think God has given me the gift of exhortation and prophecy. My prayer life is exciting and when I get together with our prayer group, we really touch heaven! I look forward to discovering how God wants to use me."

"I get so energized when our group goes out to help others. We have served in the downtown soup kitchen, built a home for Habitat for Humanity and fixed cars for single moms. Serving Christ in this way brings me such fulfillment. I have also grown very close with my small group of friends... we call our group 'Servants of the Savior.'"

"My Bible classes have really helped me get the answers I need. Having a solid theological foundation is important for every Christian. I can't believe how many Christians don't have a clue about what they really believe. There is so much deception in the world out there; God wants us to speak truth to them. I think God is calling me to teach others and to uphold sound doctrine."

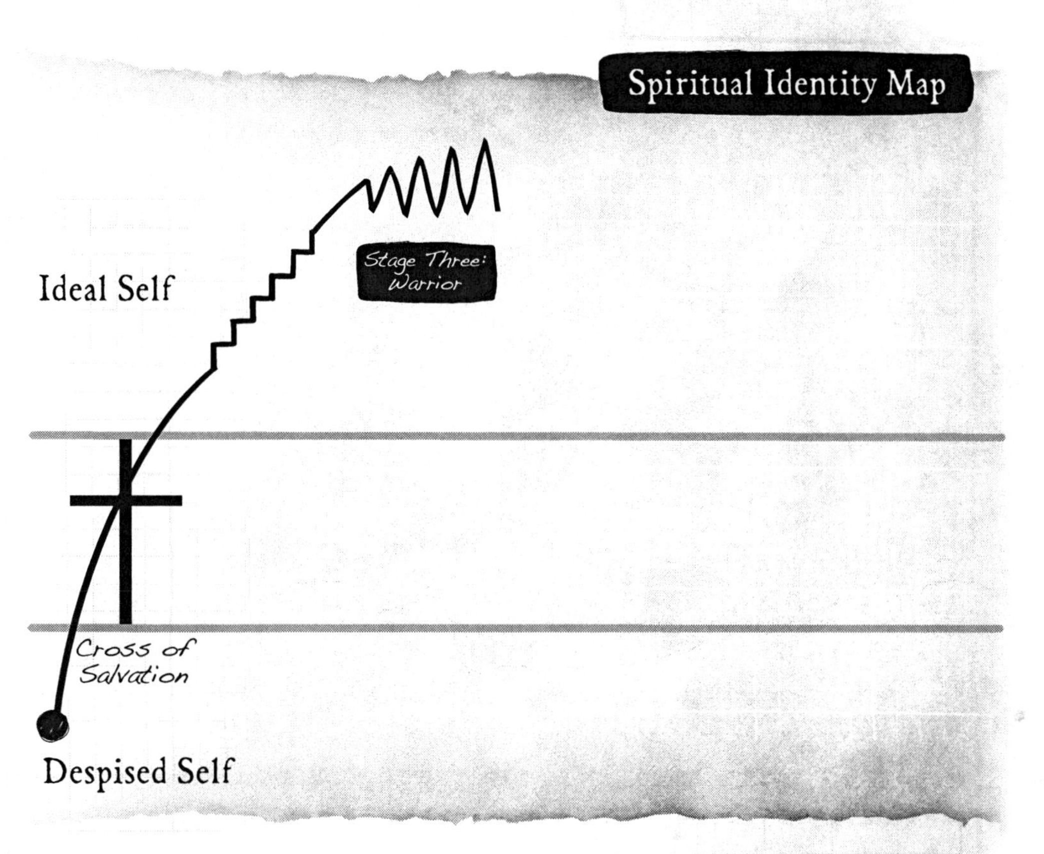

The transition from Learner to a Stage Three Warrior propels us higher into the realm of our Ideal Self. This exciting stage is about achievement, accomplishment and winning. We may take on new roles at the prodding of a leader, boss or mentor. We may feel that we are in way over our heads, but soon discover our efforts are bearing fruit. Our gifts are beginning to mature and we find strength and excitement in suiting up and taking the field.

> "The ultimate measure of a man is not where he stands in moments of comfort and convenience, but where he stands at times of challenge and controversy."
>
> — Martin Luther King Jr.

Notice that the Spiritual Identity Map pictures the Warrior's path as a series of ever-increasing spikes. These symbolize particular battles or achievements. The peaks represent our victories and the valleys represent some of our losses and defeats. A true warrior will have both, rising after each battle to fight again. King David spent a lot of his life as a warrior. At the top of his game, he proclaims: "With your help I can advance against a troop; with my God I can scale a wall" (2 Samuel 22:30).

To understand the Warrior Stage, we must broaden our concept beyond the wild, sword-wielding combatant. While this may be a part of this stage for some, there is much more to warring than that. Women, as well as men, become warriors and together we battle in the realms of academics, business, sports, marriage, politics, words and ideas, church leadership, child-raising, social action etc. Those at this stage are fully in the game and want to make a difference. There is a drive that begins boiling in our being. All the learning of Stage Two is now engaged toward a cause. This kind of productivity feeds our soul. Our ambition drives us on as we achieve one goal after another.

Passion and zeal for a cause are what properly identify the warrior. We have clear vision for our future and are confident our accomplishments will better the world. Most of our warrior years are full of optimism and seemingly endless energy. We are buoyant in spirit and our faith is strong. We go for it, knowing "If God is for us, who can be against us?" The dips on the map represent our defeats, which we consider only temporary setbacks. We are "more than conquerors" through Christ (Romans 8:31, 37)! This glorious, adrenaline-charged season can carry us for twenty to thirty years depending on God's work in us, life circumstances and our individual temperament.

This great stage of activism should not be seen as mere idealistic ambition. God has established much good in this world through its warriors. Great cathedrals have been built, injustices have been righted, laws have been passed, missions have been launched, theologies have been formed and lives have been saved. It is appropriate for us to live this stage to its fullest. In fact, it is concerning to see people who ought to be warriors living weak, uncommitted and passive lives. Sadly, our society has devalued the role of the Warrior. Robert Bly laments this void in men in particular:

> *"The warriors inside American men have become weak in recent years...a grown man six feet tall will allow another person to cross his boundaries, enter his psychic house, verbally abuse him, carry away his treasures and slam the door behind; the invaded man will stand there with an ingratiating, confused smile on his face."*

Lest you think of the Warrior Stage as only a male phenomenon, consider some of the amazing women of scripture who fought and won in a full array of battl fields: Sarah, Deborah, Rachel, Leah, Ruth, Queen Esther, Mary the mother of Jesus, and Priscilla, to name just a few. The description of the virtuous woman of Proverbs 31 paints a picture of a warring woman in the realms of family, finance, leadership, employment and character.

"A wife of noble character who can find? She is worth far more than rubies. Her husband has full confidence in her and lacks nothing of value. She brings him good, not harm, all the days of her life. She selects wool and flax and works with eager hands. She is like the merchant ships, bringing her food from afar. She gets up while it is still dark; she provides food for her family and portions for her servant girls. She considers a field and buys it; out of her earnings she plants a vineyard. She sets about her work vigorously; her arms are strong for her tasks. She sees that her trading is profitable, and her lamp does not go out at night."

— Proverbs 31:10-18

The Warrior stage is one of passion for our cause; it is about strong convictions and taking ground. For the Warrior it is all about fighting and winning. This is a glorious time in our lives as we soar high in the realms of Ideal Self. Yes, there are trials and setbacks, as shown by the dips on the map, but, like a rubber ball, we bounce back ready to take on new heights. This stage must be celebrated and lived to the full for God's glory. We should hone our skills, act strategically and take bold steps of faith without apology. While showing proper respect for our older predecessors, we must be willing to explore new frontiers and scale new heights. Yes, there will be a time for resting and reassessing, but for the Warrior, that time is NOT now! Proverbs 20:29 says, *"The* ***glory*** *of young men* ***is their strength,*** *gray hair the splendor of the old."*

Although we do not often think of our Lord this way, God Himself, is a Warrior! An honest reading of Scripture shows God as strong and mighty and willing to use His power to accomplish His will on earth. Consider Isaiah 42:13 which says, "The LORD will march out like a mighty man, like a warrior he will stir up his zeal; with a shout he will raise the battle cry and will triumph over his enemies." Further, the mission of Jesus Christ on earth was more than simply loving and healing. Can you picture Jesus filled with holy indignation turning over the tables in the temple and driving the sellers out with a whip? It was after this passionate display that, "His disciples remembered that it is written: "Zeal for your house will consume me" (John 2:17). Jesus came to make war against Satan's kingdom. 1 John 3:8b says "The reason the Son of God appeared was to destroy the devil's work." Praise God that our Savior went to war for our salvation!

NO.

DATE

Time to Reflect...

Slowly and thoughtfully trace your pen or pencil over the spikes and dips of the Warrior's experience. As you do, think of some of the things you've accomplished - some of the battles you've won. Using just a few words, label your victories at the top of the peaks.

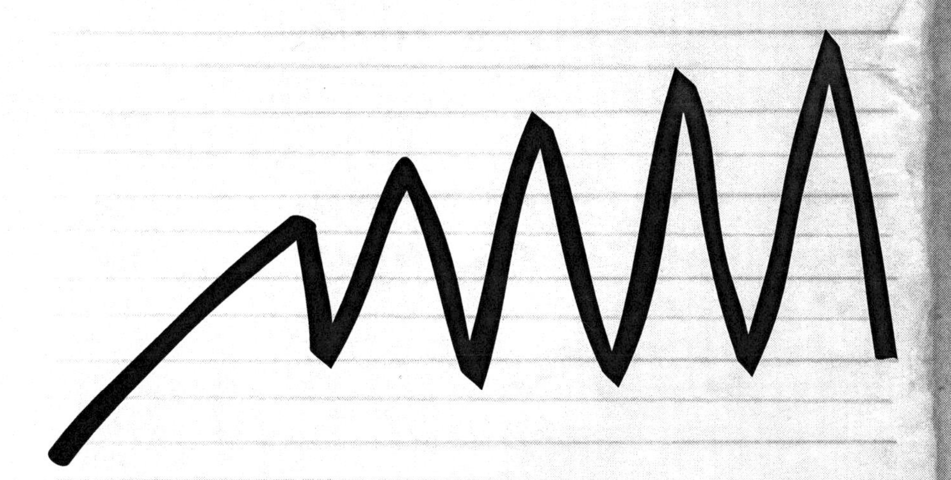

The Warrior's Achilles' Heel

For all the glories of the Stage Three Warrior there are also weaknesses. Spiritual pride can be a subtle invader as we accomplish more and more for God. Victories in our own lives can cause us to look down on others who aren't as far along as we are. We are strong in ourselves and forget that our strength comes from God and must bear His fingerprints. Students of the Bible can be so right in the "letter of the law" that they miss the "spirit of the law," failing to see that spiritual pride is subtly (or not so subtly) tainting their message.

Warriors can also get addicted to fruit-bearing and achieving. This is hard to detect when all we see is the good we are doing for our world. As far as we are concerned, if all the numbers are going up and to the right, we are winning; life is good! Meanwhile, we are completely unaware that our own soul may be in danger. Our family may be suffering as we run off, yet another night of the week, to do something good and godly. Fruit-bearing addiction can also be an drug of sorts for inner-life brokenness. For example, a son having been told by his father all his life that he's a loser may be driven to achieve more and more in his career to 'prove him wrong.'

Hard-charging Warriors commonly become insensitive to those who are hurting and needy. We are running too fast toward our own goals to see the people around who need us. Our lack of sympathy seems justified by all the progress we are making. Driven personalities are especially wired to reach for spikes of achievement. Though spoken with varying degrees of intensity, the warrior's mantra is very clear, *"Lead, follow or get out of the way!"* After all, at this stage we're almost invincible!

It took me many years of ministry to see the danger of my Warrior's sword. When I discovered that God had given me a leadership gift, I set out to lead. Opinionated and right, I worked hard to establish a growing, vibrant church. In those years, the slow were run over and the hurting were too often kicked to the curb. There was a vision to accomplish, souls to save and buildings to build! I wanted you to either run with me or step aside. My heart was in the right place most of the time, but viewing life through the narrow focus of a toilet paper tube caused me to really hurt some people. I am amazed at God's graciousness in blessing our work, even with all of my faults. He loves His church and uses imperfect humans to serve His cause on earth! I have had to make apologies over the years and hope that those around me have seen the fruit of my repentance.

Jesus nicknamed the brothers, James and John, *"Boanerges"* which means *"Sons of Thunder."* Why, do you suppose that was? I believe that it was linked to their zeal and fervency for the Gospel. But when Jesus was rejected by the Samaritans, it was James and John who asked the Lord, "Do you want us to call fire down from heaven to destroy them?" Jesus had to rebuke them. Their zeal was from a wrong spirit (Luke 9:54-55). This is often the error of godly Warriors who are right in their might, but not always in their perspective. I have worked with some *"sons of thunder"* in ministry as well - some named for their unbridled passion and some named for their skill with bodily noises!

Growing Wise in War

When we are at the top of our game in Stage Three, we think the line depicting our progress on our map will continue to rise into the stratosphere. The transition into our next stage of development can take us by surprise. It begins while we are out there achieving and accomplishing great things. Our exploits in battle, while exhilarating, begin to take their toll on us. In the words of John Dryden, "I'm wounded but am not slain, I will lay me down for to bleed a while." *(from Johnnie Armstrong's Last Goodnight)* We awaken to the reality that with battle comes bloodshed...and to our surprise much of it is our own.

There is a graphic picture of a true warrior in the story of Eleazar, one of King David's mighty men. One day while battling the Philistines, all the

Israelites but Eleazar retreated. Eleazar "stood his ground and struck down the Philistines till his hand grew tired and froze to the sword. The LORD brought about a great victory that day" (2 Sam 23:10).

There are times when, as warriors, we find ourselves standing alone in the middle of a battlefield – victorious, but bleeding and tired. In these times, we hear a voice inside us asking, *"Remind me again, why am I doing this?"* Suddenly we begin to question the purpose and meaning behind all our sword swinging. The repeated crisis and grief of war takes its toll and causes us to lose our bearings. The tendons and muscles of our soul have formed around the handle of our sword and though we may want to lay it down, we feel frozen there. For the first time in a long time, our sense of certainty and dogma is shaken; we begin to have more questions than answers. And then something we thought only happens to the weak and uncommitted begins happening to us....we'll look at that in Stage Four.

In his excellent book, *Halftime*, Bob Buford writes, "I remember reading in a Sierra Club book about the assault on the western ridge of Mount Everest. After spending millions of dollars and experiencing loss of life among their fellow climbers, two men finally reached the peak of Mount Everest. There, at the top, they viewed the world from its highest point. They had overcome enormous impediments to reach their destination, their ultimate goal, yet the emotion they experienced was not one of unadulterated elation and joyfulness. After just a few minutes, one of them began worrying about how to get down the other side before the wind blew them off the top of the mountain."

Where is God in all this achievement, warring and blood loss? Well, Warrior, He's closer than we think. The same God who wrought great exploits through us is now going to help win battles in us.

Go For It

If you are enjoying the life stage of a Warrior, I encourage you to focus all your strength on the calling that God has placed before you. You do not have to be in full-time ministry to do this, either. In whatever field of endeavor you find yourself, hold nothing back; go for it!

Release the passion and energy that God has placed within you to serve His eternal purpose. Join with other like-minded Warriors and take ground for God. Remember to also reach out to those in the earlier stages of the journey and help them along. Open your heart, mind and ears to those who have traveled farther than you have on the journey. They will give you perspective to match your passion.

Well, my sojourning friend, I hope you have your seat belt on because the next stage of the journey has been known to give whiplash to many a traveler! Do not lose heart. The Holy Spirit is still our Travel Guide. With His help we will become all He wants us to be. Perhaps He is asking a question to the Eleazar in all of us: "Can you loosen your grip on the sword?"

Going the Second Mile

Read the story of Jacob in Genesis 32:22-32. What was God's larger purpose in setting up this confrontation with this great Warrior?

Consider the battle wounds you have experienced. Which ones are still painful to this day? Why do you suppose that is?

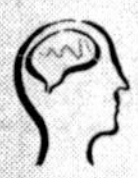

Memorize Philippians 3:7-11

Watch the gripping 1986 movie, The Mission (written by Robert Bolt and directed by Roland Joffé) about the experiences of two Jesuit missionaries in 18th century South America. Observe how two Gospel Warriors approach life. Which one are you most like?

Internet search the great hymn by Martin Luther "A Mighty Fortress is Our God." As you read the lyrics consider how you are appropriating the power of God in your life.

Stage 3 – "Warrior" Highlights

Strengths:

- *Achieving goals in God*
- *Zeal and vision in abundance*
- *Buoyant in spirit and faith*

Weaknesses:

- *Spiritual pride and self-strength*
- *Addicted to fruit-bearing*
- *Insensitive to the hurting and needy*

Moving On:

- *Reevaluating our purpose and meaning in life*
- *Blood loss from fighting helps us choose our battles more carefully*
- *Loss of bearings and grieving over a sense of powerlessness*

Life Stage Axiom:

- *"Go For It!"*

"It's in the wounding experience that I learn that I am not God, nor a little god, nor even a little bit like God. It is more the experience of wondering how or why God might have anything to do with me at all."

— Robert Hicks

When the Bottom Drops Out

Stage Four: "Brokenness"

"My tears have been my food day and night,
while men say to me all day long,
"Where is your God?" These things
I remember as I pour out my soul:
how I used to go with the multitude,
leading the procession to the house of God,
with shouts of joy and thanksgiving
among the festive throng."

— Psalm 42:3-4

"For some reason this is the most barren time in my life. I feel far from God and everyone around me. I still love God, but I have lost the zeal and passion in my faith. I don't know how to proceed. It feels like my soul is broken, never to be repaired again."

"I never thought I would lose; I only thought I'd win."
– Elton John, "The Last Song"

"Every step of my journey these days is agonizing. The more I honestly look at my soul, the more I see the junk I stuffed away 25 years ago and thought I'd never have to see again."

"How can I be a leader in our church and be in this place of such disillusionment? I feel like I'm just going through the motions."

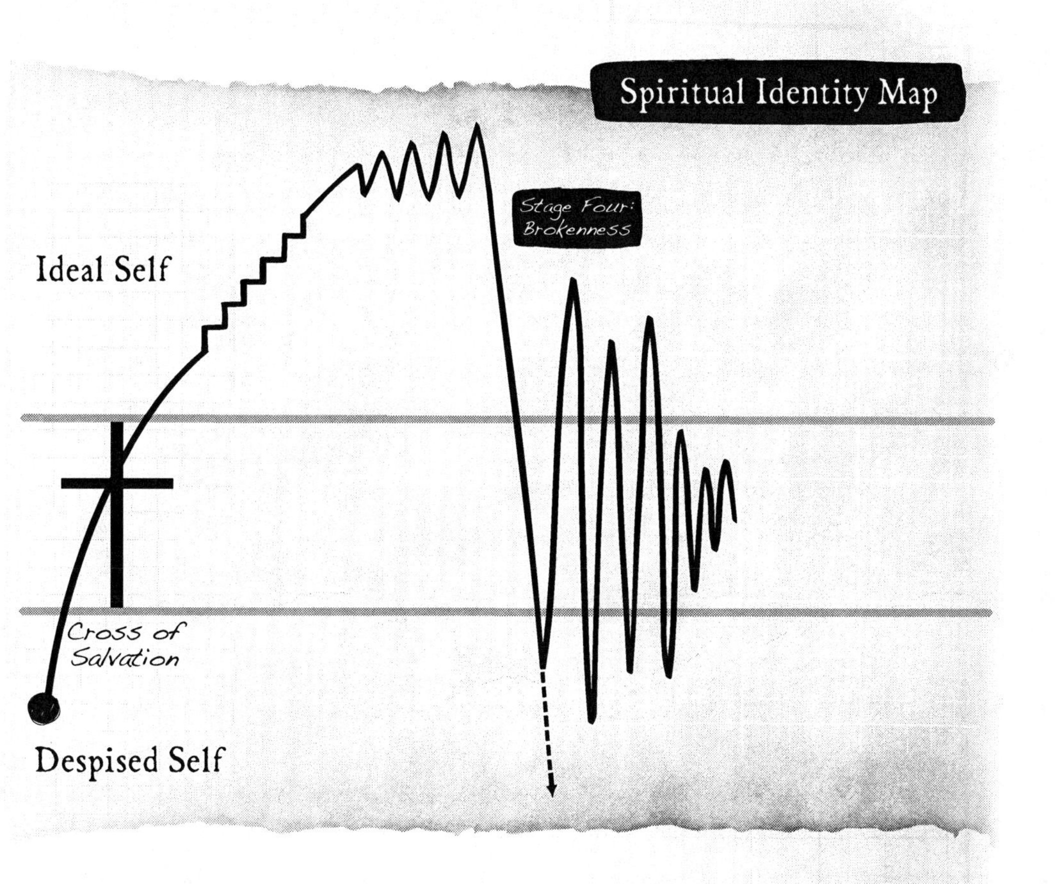

Stage Four Brokenness is perhaps the most misunderstood and painful season of our life.

It seems that everything is running smoothly and then suddenly the bottom drops out of our soul. Look at the line on the Spiritual Identity Map. Have you ever felt this way? Suddenly the only thing we can hear is the wind whistling past our ears as we fall like meteors out of the sky. Our fall isn't necessarily a moral fall into sin or spiritual backsliding. Here we may face the desperate feelings of being mad at God, hurt by others and disappointed in ourselves. This is more than one of those temporary setbacks we experienced as Stage Three Warriors. Here we drop and continue to fall.

We have more questions than answers: Is there a bottom to this free fall? Will I hit the ground and explode into a million pieces? Where is the confidence I once had? Why do I find it hard to be sure about anything anymore? Why are these old temptations rearing their ugly heads again after so many years? Worse yet, who can I talk to and admit the depth of this spiritual void that I feel? Floyd McClung describes it: "You wake up one morning and are your spiritual feelings are gone. You pray, but nothing happens. You rebuke the devil, but it doesn't change anything. You go through spiritual exercises you have your friends pray for you… you confess every sin you can imagine, then go around asking forgiveness of everyone you know. You fast… still nothing. You begin to wonder how long this spiritual gloom might last. Days? Weeks? Months? Will it ever end?… it feels as if your prayers simply bounce off the ceiling. In utter desperation, you cry out, 'What's the matter with me?'"

The dotted line on the map shows the unfortunate path of some at this stage. Their fall from the sky is so intense that they cannot (or choose not to) pull up. Picture an airplane pilot in a nose dive. Either he can pull back on the yoke with all his might, enduring the intense G-force, or he can allow his plane to plunge into the ground. Both are difficult; each is a choice we must make. The plunging line is dotted because smashing our lives into the ground is OPTIONAL! Although our feelings may tell us to crash this thing and be done with it, we must remember that the dotted line takes us back to our Despised Self and leads to death.

Two of Jesus' disciples, Judas Iscariot and Peter, both "fell out of the sky" as Jesus was walking through Passion Week. Judas betrayed Jesus for thirty pieces of silver. Peter denied three times that he even knew Jesus. Following their failures, they both had an excruciating choice to make in response to their Brokenness. Judas lost all hope of personal redemption and committed the ultimate act of hopelessness by hanging himself. Peter, on the other hand, wept in bitter disappointment at his failure. The Bible does not tell us what happened within Peter's soul in that moment, but we can only imagine the depth of grief experienced by this self-proclaimed loyal disciple (See Matthew 26:74-75; 27:5).

"When a man is pushed, tormented, defeated;
he has a chance to learn something."
— Ralph W. Emerson

For all of the confusion of Stage Four, God is giving a gift: a new level of spiritual brokenness. This is not the bad kind of brokenness such as addictions, abuse, codependency and anger issues. Brokenness at this stage is the ability to embrace our own weakness and vulnerability before an almighty God. Here we realize how much we have been running on our own soul-strength and independence.

The Apostle Paul was a man who knew how to be a warrior for God, but there was one revelation he received that changed how he viewed his battles. We read about it in 2 Corinthians 12:7-10.

> "To keep me from becoming conceited because of these surpassingly great revelations, there was given me a thorn in my flesh, a messenger of Satan, to torment me. Three times I pleaded with the Lord to take it away from me. But he said to me, "My grace is sufficient for you, for **my power is made perfect in weakness.**" Therefore I will boast all the more gladly about my weaknesses, so that Christ's power may rest on me. That is why, for Christ's sake, **I delight in weaknesses,** in insults, in hardships, in persecutions, in difficulties. **For when I am weak, then I am strong.**"

The Apostle Paul had prayed for the sick and they were healed. He had raised the dead to life by God's power. He had great faith and anointing, but there was a prayer that God would not answer for him in the way he wanted. There have been many speculations about what this "thorn in the flesh" was and I won't take time to speak to that here. But this I know: it was some form of painful adversity that Paul wanted out of his life. The Lord spoke to him and gave him a greater answer to prayer when He said, "My power is made perfect (complete, accomplished) in your weakness." As Warriors we learn to fight weakness at all costs. But, when we take the path of Brokenness we recognize that "God's grace is sufficient" for all things. And with Paul, we can begin to say that "When I am weak, then I am strong."

"We turn to God for help when our foundations are shaking,
only to learn that it is God who is shaking them."
— Charles C. West

Through this great fall we come to understand humility at a deeper level. Our compassion for others increases as we see ourselves at the same level of neediness. As Warriors we barked orders at these fallen saints, commanding them to get back up and join the fight...or else. Now we're not sure if we can (or even want to) get up ourselves!

We are sure our Warrior friends won't understand us, so we become afraid to expose our wounds. Warriors will offer glib words of advice or perhaps a well-delivered rebuke. If that doesn't work they may run us through with their sword to put us out of our misery. This is where we prove the saying true: "Christians are the only army in the world that shoots their wounded."

I was 44 years old and had been in full time ministry for over 20 years. This particular night found me coming home late after a uniquely difficult meeting. I was depressed, despondent and did not want to talk about it with my good wife, Becky. Trying to decompress, I turned on the TV (not always the best medicine, by the way) as we sat on the couch together. I was intrigued as the news anchor told of a groundbreaking report which determined both the happiest and the saddest year of life from a worldwide survey. As they went to a commercial break, I muted the sound and told Becky, "I bet the saddest year is going to be in the mid 40's." (I wasn't focused on the happiest year of life at that point.) "What do you think?" I asked her. "Oh, the saddest year is probably when people get old and sick…say in their 70's and 80's," she thoughtfully replied. The reporter came back on and began explaining the scope of this survey, building our anticipation to hear the results. Laying it out, she said, "So the saddest year of life, according to our worldwide survey, is… forty-four years old." At this, I glanced over to look at Becky to confirm my state of helpless woe and she said, "Well honey, look at it this way, it is only going to get better from here!" Indeed, it is not good for man to be alone! By the way, the happiest age was in the post-retirement golden years.

> "Why are you downcast, O my soul? Why so disturbed within me? Put your hope in God, for I will yet praise him, my Savior and my God."
>
> — Psalm 42:5-6

Humpty Dumpty had a Great Fall…

Stage Four Brokenness is a very vulnerable time for us, for while God is at work in us, our enemy the devil is also at work, trying to take advantage of this season. Our confusion and hurt tempts us to give up on God - and all of His kids.

Once, while teaching this segment to a gathering of pastors in Texas, a seasoned pastor spoke up during a question and answer session and said before the whole group, *"I know exactly what this stage feels like; now I understand what's been happening. I have been in it for ten years."* Here he was, doing the work of ministry (marrying, burying, preaching, worshiping, praying, counseling and caring for his flock), as his own soul endured this excruciating season of brokenness. I had to admire this man for his honesty and also for staying in the game. Oh, how we would like to avoid this season of pain, but we can't!

Our disappointments in Stage Four can lead us to becoming very cynical. Cynicism is a disease of the soul and spiritual cynicism is its most deadly form. We can be cynical toward our work, government, finances, even toward our marriage. But, spiritual cynicism closes the door to the very source of the help we need. In our pessimism, we can shut out God and those to whom we would have formerly looked for help. Often, because of the vagueness of this stage, even our mentors have no words for us. Trusting comes hard for us in our pain.

"Many men owe the grandeur of their lives to their tremendous difficulties."
— Charles H. Spurgeon

Having fallen from our great height, we are tempted to look back on our glorious Warrior years and write them off as a waste of time. *"What a fool I was; what was I thinking?"* is our groan. We remember all the time, energy and money we spent on accomplishing great things, only to categorize it as nothing more than youthful zeal. We forget that God, in fact, did do great things in us and through us. There is none so disillusioned as one who has lived among the shining stars of heaven only to fall to the swamp of earth - having been conquered by the inevitability of mortal gravity.

"I am now the most miserable man living... Whether I shall ever be better, I cannot tell. I awfully forebode I shall not."
— Abraham Lincoln, Letter to John T. Stuart, January 23, 1841

I must make something very clear at this point: our big fall is NOT spiritual backsliding. It does not make us discipleship dropouts. Some onlookers may misinterpret what is happening in our lives as spiritual regression. Rather, it is coming to grips with the fact that living in our Ideal

Self is not a perpetual reality! The experience of "Brokenness" is actually a *coming home* to a new authenticity in Christ. We begin to see the realms of both our Despised Self and our Ideal Self in a new light. In days past it was easy to see our Despised Self as a state of bondage. We now realize that the realm of our Ideal Self can also be a place of bondage of sorts. This is not a bondage to overt sin, but a bondage to self: self-strength, self-ambition, self-promotion, self-sufficiency. This awakening can be jarring to the soul, but grasping it enables us to begin living in what I term our Authentic Self. We will discuss the power of this new realm in the next chapter.

A closer look at the Apostle Peter's life shows us that God is very much at work in us during this time. Jesus told him, "Simon, Simon, Satan has asked to sift you as wheat. But I have prayed for you, Simon, that your faith may not fail. And when you have turned back, strengthen your brothers" (Luke 22:31-32). Note that Jesus does not tell Peter that He'd keep the devil from sifting him. Rather He prays for him to survive the ordeal so that he can come out purified. It is only after this kind of dealing that we can truly "strengthen the brothers," yet how many of us are willing to pay this price?

In his outstanding book, *Courageous Leadership,* Bill Hybels talks openly about when his bottom dropped out. "I remember sitting in a restaurant and writing: 'The pace at which I've been doing the work of God is destroying God's work in me.' Then, still sitting in that restaurant, I put my head down on my spiral notebook and sobbed. After mopping up, I said, 'God, what's going on here?' I sensed the Holy Spirit saying, 'Bill, who has a gun to your head? Who is intimidating you into overcommitting? Whose approval and affirmation and applause other than God's are you seeking? What makes you live this way?' The answers were worse than sobering. They were devastating."

Stage Four Brokenness is a time of reevaluating and coming to grips with some of those hidden things that have driven our lives for the last couple of decades. For as painful as this is, it is a work of God's grace in our lives - not to leave us devastated, but to give us a new footing for the next few decades of life!

Time to Reflect...

NOTE

DATE

- Read Lamentations 3:25-33. What parts of this experience can you relate to personally?

- Mother Teresa once said, "I am told God loves me and yet the reality of darkness and coldness and emptiness is so great that nothing touches my soul." Write down the place and circumstance in your life that left you feeling this way.

NO.

DATE

- In times of brokenness it is important to give words to what we are feeling. Circle any of the words below that describe this time in your life:

Angry	Confused	Abandoned
Hurt	Misunderstood	Accused
Unsure	Lonely	Weak
Hopeless	Numb	Disappointed
Blind	Vulnerable	Depressed
Unmotivated	Caged	Aggressive
Uncaring	Nostalgic	Regretful
Dependent	Embarrassed	Out of Control

Making Progress in Our Pain

During this time of Brokenness we are desperate to regain some sense of stability and familiarity. Notice the line on the map bounces between the realms of Ideal Self and Despised Self. It even crosses the lines back into these realms. This is to illustrate our propensity for extreme behavior during this time. Some days we feel like we are carried along by angels and able to recover the heights of Ideal Self. Other days we are convinced that we are demon-possessed and totally defeated in sin. It's as if we're wearing a steel jacket and trying to walk between two huge electromagnets, pulling us back and forth between the two realms! On one hand we want to regain our old glory, spiritual strength and confidence. On the other hand we are tempted to self-medicate on the old sins of our Despised Self. Indeed, this is a perilous season of vulnerability of soul. Sadly, some of our traveling buddies don't survive this stage.

However, immeasurable benefit comes from this stage when we can see the hand of God in it. This is a crucible of purification. It is where our human will is invited to find perfect submission and rest in God. The discipline of the Lord is brought to bear in the hidden places of our lives. Like children, we can either buck discipline or benefit from it. Hebrews 12:5-6 exhorts us to stay centered as God does His loving work. We must neither lose heart nor make light of it.

"My son, do not **make light** of the Lord's discipline, and do not **lose heart** when he rebukes you, because the Lord disciplines those he loves, and he punishes everyone he accepts as a son."

— Hebrews 12:5-6

Author Gary Thomas writes in *The Beautiful Fight* about this inner spiritual brokenness: "If I recognize that I am not like Christ, that I am proud where he is humble, that I am selfish where he is sacrificial, that I am greedy where he is giving, that I am lustful where he is pure, then mustn't I be broken before I can be remade? Of course I must. And so must you. The breaking can be painful, even excruciating. It hurts to die to certain dreams and desires. It sometimes feels as though we're being ripped apart when we let something go. But the pain is a *good* pain, the difficult journey is a *good* journey, and the Beautiful Fight is still a *beautiful* fight."

One of the best balms for our wounded soul at this time is to find a friend who has gone through this stage and has come out healthy and healed. Look for someone who has suffered pain and processed it well. Ask them about their story. Tell them yours. They can serve as guardrails for our soul to keep us from driving our lives into a ditch. We must allow ourselves to grieve the loss of our former strength and forgive those who may have offended us. Our friend will remind us that there will be new strength in days to come. We would do well to believe them and take hope in God's faithfulness.

In an interesting study throughout their many wars, the Israeli Mental Health Corps has learned why wounded Israeli soldiers heal faster than U.S. soldiers. If a U.S. soldier gets wounded in battle, they are airlifted out of the war zone to a medical hospital, stripped of their uniform and placed in a white hospital gown. This seems like a sensible and medically beneficial approach. This is not the experience of a wounded Israeli soldier. They keep their wounded with their combat units, doing everything medically possible for them while still in the war zone. Although wounded, the soldier is left in his uniform. Even with amputated limbs and loss of basic functions, he is still seen as a functioning soldier. Amazingly, the wounded Israeli soldier is found in uniform, surrounded by his fellow soldiers. They value the warrior even when wounded. If we learn to honor those in deep Brokenness in this way, they will recover sooner and with a sense of hope and dignity.

While our wounds may not be physical, we have those around us with holes blown through their soul, bullet holes in their confidence and vision loss due to explosive trauma. What will we do with our wounded Warriors?

Will we give them time to heal and affirm their God-given identity? Will we keep them near us or will we be repulsed by their wounds?

"It is in the quiet crucible of your personal, private sufferings
that your noblest dreams are born and God's greatest gifts are given
in compensation for what you have been through."
— Wintley Phipps

Hang On - Don't Give Up

Well, how are you doing, traveling companion? This stage feels like the drop of a giant roller coaster, although not nearly as much fun! If you find yourself in Stage Four Brokenness, my encouragement to you is to stay in the journey. Your discouragement may be so intense that you are looking for relief from anywhere. You may want to run, give up or give in…don't! Take some time for solitude. Get before God and pour your heart out to him. Open the Psalms and make them your prayers. Find a safe person with whom you can share your inner life. Keep in mind that it's best to not make any major life-altering decisions when you are in this place. There are better days ahead for you even if everything is screaming the opposite. My friend, our biggest battles are won, not by our show of strength, but by our endurance and tenacity.

Because this is such a critical leg of our journey, we need to pause and look at another aspect of this stage. It deals with the two "electromagnets" I referred to earlier and will be the topic of discussion in our next chapter. Godly brokenness requires a level of surrender to which our human will is often averse. Let's embrace Christ and his dealings even more fully as we travel on together. The road ahead still looks a bit treacherous. Do you want to pull over and rest for a while?

Going the Second Mile

Read Hebrews 12:5-11. How have you been responding to the discipline of the Lord in your life? What have you learned?

Read the following quote from educator and author, Parker Palmer and consider what some of your "shadowy places" might be.

"There's a lot of fear connected with the inner journey because it penetrates our illusions. Taking the inner journey will lead you into some very shadowy places. You're going to learn things about yourself that you'll wish you didn't know. There are monsters in there—monsters you can't control—but trying to keep them hidden will only give them greater power." — Parker Palmer, Leader to Leader Fall 2001

Memorize an important passage for those in Stage Four Brokenness from Hebrews 10:35-39.

Watch the 1997 movie, "The Apostle" for a vivid example of a church leader in Brokenness. Note: this film is rated PG-13 and may not be appropriate for sensitive viewers.

Read Jonah chapter 2 and underline the phrases that speak to you. Now make them a prayer back to God.

To discover how another Christian leader has handled Stage Four, read Pastor Wayne Cordeiro's book, "Leading on Empty" (Bethany House).

Find the lyrics for the hymn "Tis so Sweet to Trust in Jesus" by Louisa M. R. Stead. The author penned these amazing words in one of her darkest hours. She and her daughter had just witnessed the drowning of her husband as he was attempting to save the life of a boy who also drowned in the ocean. It was out of her struggle with God during the ensuing days that these meaningful words flowed -"Tis so sweet to trust in Jesus."

Stage 4 – "Brokenness" Highlights

Strengths:

- *Learning to embrace weakness*
- *A new understanding of humility*
- *Gaining compassion for others*

Weaknesses:

- *Giving up on God and others, isolation*
- *Becoming spiritually cynical*
- *Categorizing your past as a waste*

Moving On:

- *Resist the retreat toward your "Despised Self" or "Ideal Self"*
- *Submit to God's discipline*
- *Relate to those who have suffered well*

Life Stage Axiom:

- *"Hang On ` Don't Give Up"*

Notes

7

The Futility of Stuckness

Avoiding Life's Parking Lots

"The greatest difficulty in conversion
is to win the heart to God,
and the greatest difficulty after conversion
is to keep the heart with God."

—John Flavel, seventeenth-century Puritan

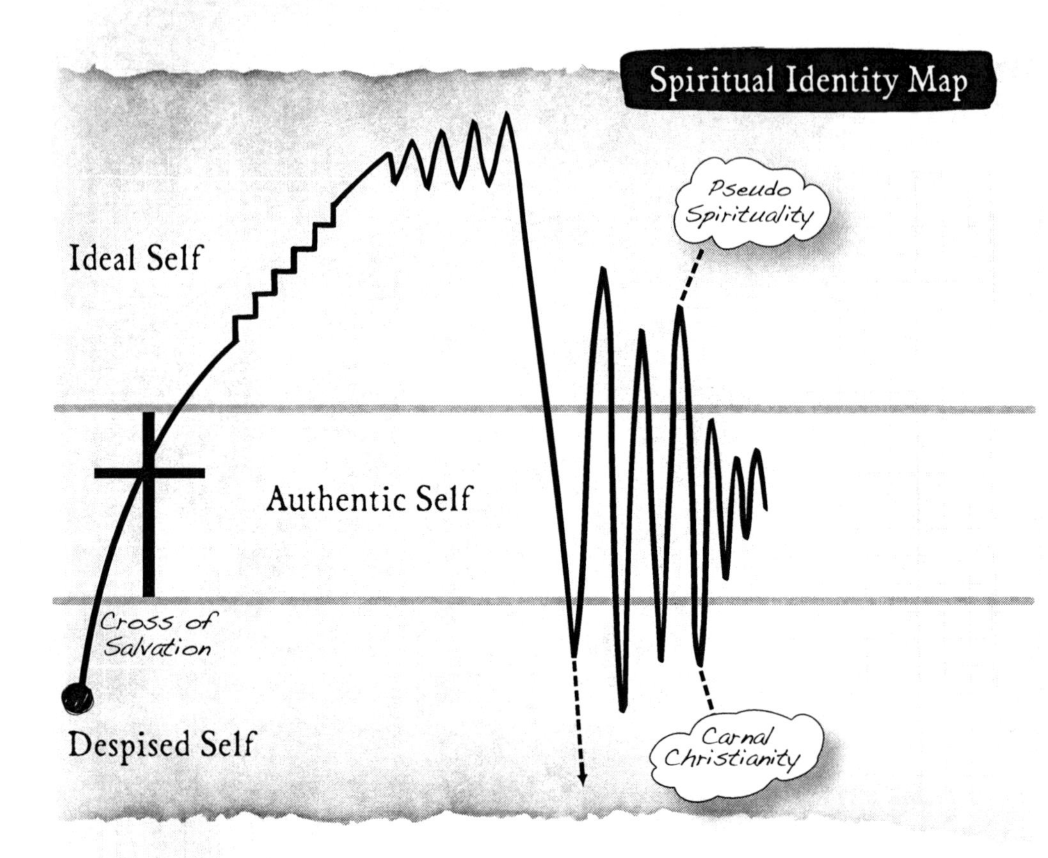

This chapter does not deal with a new stage in our developmental process. Rather it describes two potential places for the traveler to get stuck; we will call them parking lots. A parking lot represents a stopping place. When our engines are off and our cars are in park, we are not moving. This kind of stopping is not for the appropriate potty break and timely refueling. These two parking lots are all about escape, avoidance, self-deception and pretending. Hanging out here can literally jeopardize whether we complete our journey as God has planned. Thus the wise traveler must identify and avoid these stuck places. As we examine these two parking lots, take note that they are polar opposites. I identify them as *Carnal Christianity* and *Pseudo Spirituality.*

Carnal Christianity is where a traveler becomes sidetracked by sinful choices, behaviors and attitudes. The intense nature of Stage Four causes some Christians to self-medicate with old sinful practices and escapist behaviors. Addictions can form (or reform) here and take the traveler on a sinister slide of self-destruction. Here they hope that they are still in God's good graces while they indulge their selfish cravings. They have a foot in the world and a foot in the Kingdom of God. Carnality here can be manifest in many ways: bitterness, resentment, unforgiveness, rebellion, lust, greed, worldly pursuits, anger, unbelief and stubbornness. While this person may still want to "fellowship" with other Christians and attend church regularly, they have chosen to resist the inner dealings of God. They have denied the very grace of God needed to change and have slid into spiritual mediocrity. Often people get disappointed with God and disillusioned with the Church as they experience the deep brokenness of Stage Four. Some came to Christ because they were looking for a way out of the slime of Despised Self. This arrangement eased their pain in the early stages, but when they discover that they cannot maintain living in Ideal Self, they are once again confronted with their old inner life issues. While this is a great opportunity for inner healing, the pain is so raw that they often retreat from God's dealing into Carnal Christianity. Bible Teacher, Bill Gothard wisely describes this subtle deception when he says, "We adjust our theology to fit our morality."

This can be seen in an incident the Apostle Peter had with a man named Simon the sorcerer. Many from Samaria believed the Gospel as Phillip preached the good news. Even Simon, who was acclaimed as having great occult power, believed and was baptized! Being impressed with the power of the Holy Spirit working through Peter and John, he offered them money to possess the gifts operating in them. With clear discernment and anointed conviction, Peter rebuked him saying, "You have no part or share in this ministry, because **your heart is not right before God.** Repent of this wickedness and pray to the Lord. Perhaps he will forgive you for having such a thought in your heart. For I see that **you are full of bitterness and captive to sin**" (Acts 8:21-23). Simon's unwillingness to submit the hidden places of his heart had him stuck in the parking lot of Carnal Christianity. Such a place disqualified him from any part or share in the Gospel ministry, in spite of his spiritual sounding aspirations.

The other potential place of stuckness is the parking lot we call Pseudo Spirituality. This is a bit harder to describe because it can look so "good" by all outward appearance. People in this place get off the path of God's dealings and launch into a Never-Never Land of self-contrived spirituality. They want you to be impressed with their spiritual insights, visions and angelic sightings. These people may, in fact, have authentic, charismatic gifts with which they bless the body of Christ, but when it is mixed with avoidance of Brokenness, something sick sets into their soul. They suffer from what I call a "spirit of weirdness." They love to gather other people around themselves to affirm their spirituality. Sadly, these good people are part of what some pastors have come to call the *Granola Crowd* – an assortment of fruits, flakes and nuts!

"So do not throw away your confidence; it will be richly rewarded. You need to persevere so that when you have done the will of God, you will receive what he has promised. For in just a very little while, 'He who is coming will come and will not delay. But my righteous one will live by faith. And if he shrinks back, I will not be pleased with him.'
But we are not of those who shrink back and are destroyed,
but of those who believe and are saved."
— Hebrews 10:35-39

A common symptom of those parked in this place is that they reject all forms of spiritual authority. Other people stuck in Pseudo Spirituality are longing for the good old days of their former life stages. They are particularly fond of reliving their Learner and Warrior years. This can be manifest in a kind of sacred sentimentality which demands the songs, sermons and expressions of days gone by. For some, the pain and confusion of Stage Four Brokenness does not compute with their faith confession. They have no theological grid for suffering. They want God to work for them as He did in the past, so they launch into a realm of spiritual unreality. Being self-convinced that God is anointing them, they are able to avoid what He is really after in them. Instead of choosing to rest and submit to God's forming hand, they construct artificial ways of relating to God as a matter of emotional survival.

I believe that the Apostle Paul was addressing this when he warned the church at Colossae, "Do not let anyone who delights in **false humility** and the **worship of angels** disqualify you for the prize. Such a person goes into **great detail** about what he has seen, and his **unspiritual mind** puffs him up with **idle notions**" (Colossians 2:18). Later he warned Timothy, "The time will come when men will not put up with sound doctrine. Instead, to suit their own desires, they will gather around them a great number of teachers to say what their itching ears want to hear. They will turn their ears away from the truth and turn aside to myths" (2 Timothy 4:3-4).

So, how are we to respond to God at this time in our journey? Notice on the map that there is a funneling down of the bouncing line. God is orchestrating this movement to tame our inner lives; He is leading us somewhere. He is after the totality of our soul (our mind, will and emotions.) We could say that in the Learner Stage our MIND was most impacted. In the Warrior Stage our EMOTIONS were engaged. Now in the Brokenness stage, our WILL is being dealt with. God is working to corral our wayward will into submission and to bring us into a whole new level of self-awareness. The intensity of this dealing can be so concentrated that some opt out and choose to pull off into one of the two parking lots. In so doing, they deny the riches that Christ is offering and give themselves over to demonic strongholds.

"It is funny how mortals always picture us [demons] as putting things into their minds; in reality, our best work is done by keeping things out."

— C.S. Lewis (Screwtape Letters)

It is in Stage Four that Philippians 2:12-13 comes alive in a whole new way. It says, "Therefore, my dear friends, as you have always obeyed-not only in my presence, but now much more in my absence - continue to work out your salvation with fear and trembling, for it is God who works in you to will and to act according to his good purpose."

The Apostle Paul was commending the Philippians for their obedience to Christ while he was away from them. Similarly, as parents, we want our children to obey us when we are watching them, but how much more important is it for them to obey us when we leave them at home alone? Our obedience to Christ is not proven at church, but when no one is around. It is said that character is who you are when no one is watching.

The Apostle Paul goes on to say that we are to "work out our salvation." This is the working out of the life of Christ that God has worked into us. It is working to cooperate with God and stay on the path of life transformation. It is putting sweat into the practical walking out of our salvation.

Notice also that we are to process our spirituality with "fear and trembling." Let me ask you, ***when was the last time you had fear and trembling over the work of God in your life?*** This kind of approach seems foreign to our view of spiritual development today. However, I believe that God wants us to intensely apply ourselves to how we submit to His dealings within us. If the Holy Spirit is touching an area of our lives or leading us in a particular way, we must respond in godly fear and earnestness. "For it is God who works in you…" In this season of Brokenness, we might think that it's our boss, our spouse, our pastor, circumstance of life or our financial situation that is at work. No, God is behind the scenes laboring to harness our heart toward His purpose. If He is using any of these, we must humbly receive it as from His sovereign hand. "To will and to act according to His good purpose" means that He is working in us to want to (will) and to follow through (act) for the advancement of His Kingdom. He is after our willing obedience in order that we may serve His eternal purpose on earth. This, at the end of the day, is our highest calling, isn't it?

NO.
DATE

Time to Reflect...

- In your season of Brokenness, which of the two parking lots are you drawn to the most: "Carnal Christianity" or "Pseudo Spirituality" and why?

- What are some behaviors or attitudes that you exhibit while in your parking lot?

Discovering Your Authentic Self

You may have noticed on the map that we have identified the space between the lines as *Authentic Self.* This is a new realm which is totally different from our Despised Self and Ideal Self. Understanding these three realms of identity is critical if we are to successfully navigate our *Journey to Authenticity.* As we have said before, Despised Self holds us in bondage to sin. Ideal Self holds us in bondage to *self.* But it is in the tension between these two zones that we arrive at an understanding of our Authentic Self. God has been patiently working to introduce us to this place. For it is here that God manifests Himself through us in all of our uniqueness.

This mysterious awakening is not a rebellion from all that we have known. Rather, it is a coming home to the core of who God has uniquely made us to be. It is the season of life when we begin to 'find our legs' as it were. We have experienced enough of life taking up the values of others; now we are able to begin to feel at home in our own skin. Robert Hicks calls this the quality of "differentiation." He writes:

"Differentiation…may relate to those times when I feel I am being pushed into someone else's agenda, or being pressed to respond to another's dream for my life, or having to be someone I am not. It may relate to the kind of bosses, mentors, or pastors I have had in the past. It is so easy to think that the way they did it was the right way or the only way. At some point, I believe that our careers and entire approaches to life need to be scrutinized to see if we are doing no more than trying to emulate someone we admire or doing the opposite of someone we despise. Until we reject both as 'not being me,' they hold a hellish power over our souls and we will never be the rulers of our own spirits."

Discovering our Authentic Self does not mean that we were unauthentic in our former stages. Our former stages were fitting for where we were on our journey. For example, it is appropriate for a learner to find their identity in what they are learning. For them, the realm of the Ideal Self is not unauthentic, but a particular lens through which they view life at that time. Similarly, the Warrior is being true to himself or herself as they fight for their cause. They are being genuine to their place on the map at that time. The validity of each life stage should not be diminished. But, by traveling into Stage Four and responding properly to the lessons of Brokenness, we will begin discovering something new within ourselves. This discovery is not based on what we *know* or what we *do*. It is deeper; it is based on who we *are*. Here, we begin finding the God-given elements of Authentic Self.

We may be tempted to feel like Authentic Self is a place of lukewarm Christianity because we are not running with the stallions any longer. Nothing could be further from the truth, for in this realm we find a deep and settled faith that can say with the Apostle Paul, "Christ in *me*, the hope of glory" (Colossians 1:27)! Here we find that the *real life of Christ* desires to be expressed in the *real us!* Here we discover a faith we can live with, not in mediocrity, but in the spiritual power that comes from full authenticity.

The Work of Getting Unstuck

I will never forget the night we went boating up the Mississippi River with our friends, the Miller family. We spent the day pulling our kids on tubes, swimming, sitting on the beach and cooking out. Now it was getting dark and time for us to be heading home. Navigating on the Mississippi River requires you to keep your boat in the main channel by staying in between the green and red buoys. With a proper floodlight you can zip along, even in the dark, by illuminating the buoys. The problem was that we were still many miles from home and the battery in my floodlight was running low. Rounding a bend near Minneiska, Minnesota, my floodlight cut out completely. I headed for the last buoy I saw. (Getting disoriented on the Mighty Mississippi is very dangerous.) With the Millers behind us, also without a light, we were cruising along at about 35 miles per hour in what I thought was the main channel. Suddenly, our boat came to a jarring stop and our kids and gear came sliding to the front. We had run aground on a sandbar. What I thought was fifteen feet of water was actually five inches! Thankfully no one was hurt and the Millers were able to stop their boat before running into the back of us! Becky and I, with our two oldest kids, stepped out of the boat into the dark waters. It was then we realized that it was only ankle deep! With strong pushing and slow trolling we were able to get ourselves out of that mess and back home by midnight! I learned that day that it is extremely unsettling to think you are going somewhere great when, in reality, you are off course and stuck!

If you find yourself in a stuck place it is time to get out of the boat and start pushing. God will help you get reoriented. It is as if I can hear the Family of God calling out to you from across the waters, *"Come back to us, we love you! We care for you and we want you to live out God's best."* Friend, I know your strength is small, but as you begin to take your first steps, God will rush in to help you. Here are some practical steps to help you get unstuck:

1. **Acknowledge that you may be in a self-induced place of spiritual stuckness.** Whether in Pseudo Spirituality or Carnal Christianity, you must be brutally honest with your state of being. The front door to freedom is the ability to embrace the truth.

2. **Identify the issues of your life in which you are avoiding transformation.** There are reasons why you are in a parking lot. Fear, laziness, a false view of God, stubbornness, self-indulgence, strongholds of sin, image management and deception may be some issues. Do some soul-searching and ask God to show you why you left the path. Seek input from a counselor, pastor or good friend.

3. **Repent of your life choices and submit your will to God afresh.** Repentance is a change of thinking followed by a change in behavior. Great spiritual power is released when we come to Christ Jesus in humility. Identify your self-will and relinquish all control to God. Receive Christ's forgiveness and forgive yourself. Tell the Lord that He will find a willing "yes" in your heart, wherever He leads.

4. **Begin to explore the realms of your Authentic Self.** God has a better way for you to live. One of the best things to come out of our Stage Four Brokenness experience is the discovery of our Authentic Self. Do not be afraid of what you find; explore a bit! It is not selfish to find your unique fingerprint in God. Being honest with God and others can be intimidating, but this may be your on-ramp to a new life in God. He has gifts for you to open that will bring you into a whole new fulfillment in life. It is like Christmas time for the soul!

5. **Share your discoveries with a mentor or accountability friend and ask for feedback.** Great wisdom can be gleaned when a wise friend reflects what they see in you. Stepping into your Authentic Self can give you a great sense of clarity, freedom and release. However, some of your discoveries may need to be balanced and tempered to keep you from extremes. Like an excited new driver, you might be all over the road. An honest mentor will help keep you in your appropriate lane and out of the two ditches of either Carnal Christianity or Pseudo Spirituality.

Our journey will continue as we move into Stage Five. All that has happened within us through Brokenness has prepared us for what is ahead. Allow the lessons we have learned and the grace we have received to guide you. I wish that I could tell you that it is going to be clear sailing from here on out, but I can't. The next stage on our journey will bring us closer to our Savior than ever before. I will not be able to go with you all the way on this one, but you will have the company of One who has been there before to help you.

"Blessed is the man who perseveres under trial,
because when he has stood the test, he will receive the crown of life
that God has promised to those who love him."
—James 1:12

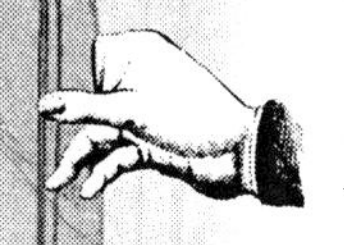

Going the Second Mile

Read the gripping prophetic message to God's people in Isaiah 30:15-22 and draw out the principles of how God helps us to get out of our parking lots.

Internet search: "The Harness of the Lord" by Bill Britton. Read this prophetic story and discuss it with a fellow traveler.

Who in your life has visited one of these stuck places and was able to get out? Call them or sit down with them and ask them about their journey.

Read Psalm 69:1-2 and personalize it as a prayer to God.

Consider this quote from British historian and cultural theorist, Arnold Toynbee (1889-1975) and list some of the ways in which God has brought (or attempted to bring) "self-mortification" into your life.

> "Unless we can bear self-mortification, we shall not be able to carry self-examination to the necessary painful lengths. Without humility there can be no illuminating self-knowledge."

Read the powerful message in the lyrics of the classic hymn "Trust and Obey" by John H. Sammis Which one of the five verses speaks to your situation right now?

Notes

"When all around us the air is full of vague rumors of a newfound faith which is free of effort and tolerant of everything save toil and pain, it is time to speak out boldly and to say that true Christianity is the most costly possession in the world, that it still knows but one road which leads over Calvary, and still has but one symbol, which is a cross."

— R. Somerset Ward

8 The Grace to Let Go

Stage Five: "Surrender"

"If anyone would come after me,
he must deny himself and
take up his cross daily and follow me.
For whoever wants to save his life will lose it,
but whoever loses his life for me will save it."

— Luke 9:23-24

"I feel very alone in my Christian walk right now. I haven't even had words to explain the pain and confusion in my soul. Some of my closest friends have been critical and judgmental; it seems that no one understands me. Rather than trying to help me up, they kicked me in the ribs and walked away! All I can pray is 'Father, forgive them for they don't know what they are doing.'"

"I never really knew before what it meant to embrace weakness. Sure, at certain times I've had to let go and surrender my will to God, but this season seems to be life-encompassing. God seems to be asking me to relinquish all of my self-strength. Like falling limp into my Father's strong arms, I just have to trust that He will take care of me."

"My life has always been marked by independence. I loved to choose my own course and go for it. But lately God has taken all of that away from me. I find myself desiring to be led by others. I ask for their input for even small steps. Their wisdom has kept me from making some very foolish mistakes. Sometimes I think that I am becoming passive, but then God reminds me that this is what obedience looks like for me."

"The last ten years have left me totally broken and weak. I have given up trying to squirm out of this uncomfortable place. It seems that God is leading me across a threshold of sorts – a finish line. I'm not sure if this is the end of my life or the beginning of something new. May His will be done."

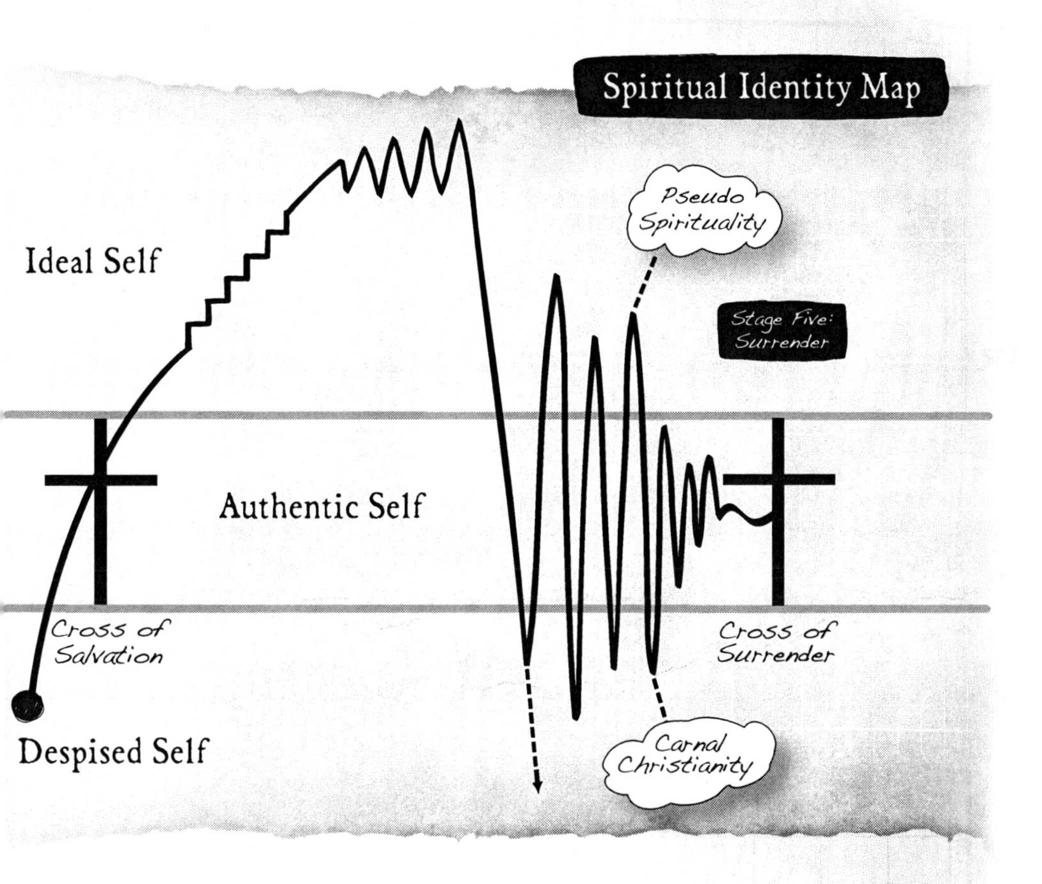

In Stage Five Surrender, we discover a second cross on the map. The first represents our Cross of Salvation, the place where we received what Jesus did for us. The second is our Cross of Surrender. The first cross was applied to Christ; the second cross is applied to us. This is the place where we willingly submit to the process of brokenness He has been working in us. Obviously, the Cross of Surrender is not to put us to death physically. Rather, it strikes our propensity to act as sovereign agents of our soul. Five times in the Gospels we hear Jesus requiring His followers to take up *their* cross and follow Him. (Matthew 10:38; 16:24, Mark 8:34, Luke 9:23; 14:27) Just as the Cross of Salvation was absolutely necessary for our New Life, so the Cross of Surrender is necessary for our progress into a new place in God.

In fact, all of God's dealings in Stage Four Brokenness have led us to this point. If we find ourselves here, it means that we have rejected (or come out of) the parking lots of life. That's worth celebrating! In many respects, this is the culminating point of what God has been trying to work in us. Yet the Cross of Surrender is not a one day experience, nor is it a onetime occurrence. From this season we take with us a pattern of surrender that we must apply to our soul *daily*. God will not allow our experience with the cross to be rushed, for each prolonged moment that we hang there, He allows yet another drop of blood to fall from our self life.

I have likened this stage to being squeezed through a knothole. We would not be able to fit through this very small space unless we had allowed the stripping away that came in Stage Four. We are no longer big in ourselves. The Holy Spirit has brought us to a place of humility and responsiveness to His will. One could say that we have dropped our sword, our books, gifts and our ambitions only to stand uncovered before our Creator. While it would have been impossible to fit through the knothole in prior stages, it is exactly where Jesus is leading us now.

"We must accept finite disappointment, but never lose infinite hope."
— Martin Luther King Jr.

A large part of this stage is finding the grace to surrender our will to God. I was told as a teenager that including *"not my will, but yours be done"* in my prayers, signified a lack of faith. My teachers thought it gave God a back door for our request. I have come to learn that this prayer is, in fact, the most faith-filled prayer we can pray. It was in the Garden of Gethsemane that Jesus prayed these very words as He was facing the reality of His cross. Only when we have come to the place of surrendered will, can we offer up this same prayer in all of its power.

The epistles of the New Testament refer to the spiritual dynamic of entering into the sufferings of Christ. It is at Stage Five that we begin to understand what they were talking about. Consider the Apostle Peter's appeal, "Dear friends, do not be surprised at the painful trial you are suffering, as though something strange were happening to you. But rejoice that you **participate in the sufferings of Christ,** so that you may be overjoyed when his glory is revealed" (1 Peter 4:12-13).

Early in our journey, all we wanted was to *learn* of Christ and His ways. Then we grew into an appreciation for His *power* working through us. The implications of following Christ on the Via Dolorosa (way of suffering) were the furthest thing from our minds. Now with the Apostle Paul we can pray, "I want to know Christ and the power of his resurrection and the fellowship of sharing in his sufferings, becoming like him in his death, and so, somehow, to attain to the resurrection from the dead." Note that he lifts up the virtues of "knowing Christ" and the "power of His resurrection," but he marries them to the reality of "sharing in his sufferings" and "becoming like him in his death" (Philippians 3:10-11).

"Those things that hurt, instruct."
— Benjamin Franklin

In their book, *The Critical Journey,* Janet Hagberg and Robert Guelich call this experience "The Wall." They explain this mystical passage, "The Wall invites us to integrate our spiritual selves with the rest of us. And that involves facing our own and others' demons. We must face that which we fear the most, and that is why it is so unsavory, and why so many people only enter the Wall under duress. At the Wall we are usually asked to embrace our illnesses and addictions and to relinquish that which we've clung to or which we worship. We encounter oceans of unresolved grief covered by anger, bitterness, martyrdom, hurt, or fear. The Wall is a place where we confront the desire to deny or disguise the inner self and begin to mentor the true self – the self God intended for us – and recognize the meaning of our shadow."

One day I was meditating on my journey and knew that God was bringing me very close to my Cross of Surrender. To be honest, it was a foreboding feeling. Then God spoke something very precious to my heart, *I will be just as real to you at your cross as I was to you when you came to My cross.* Only Jesus would know the intimacy of that place in my closet when I was just five years old. It was there my heart melted in His grace as I knelt before His cross. His renewed promise gave me great comfort and assurance as I journeyed on from there.

In Surrender we begin to realize that weakness is not our enemy, but our friend. No longer is weakness to be avoided, but embraced, for in it, we find new spiritual strength. When our strength is gone, we rely solely on the supernatural strength of God. When we cannot rescue ourselves, it has to be God's mighty intervention. When we refuse to defend ourselves, we trust in God's vindication to see us through. All of this is a new level of God's amazing grace manifested in our lives.

"The happiest people I know are the ones who have learned
how to hold everything loosely and have given the worrisome,
stress-filled,fearful details of their lives into God's keeping."
— Charles R. Swindoll

King David, the sweet psalmist of Israel, knew the soul-wrenching pain of Surrender. Author Gene Edwards writes in *A Tale of Three Kings* of him, "There in those caves, drowned in the sorrow of his song and in the song of his sorrow, David became the greatest hymn writer and the greatest comforter of broken hearts this world shall ever know."

Becoming Like Him...in His Death

Two Roman citizens were watching the gruesome martyrdom of Christians at the great Coliseum in Rome. As if at a sporting event, the crowd cheered wildly as the lions were released. Charging at their helpless prey, they began to tear at the flesh of the Christians as they knelt in prayer on the dusty floor of the Coliseum. As the dreadful climax of bloodshed was complete, one Roman spectator leaned over and commented to the other above the din of the crowd, *"My, these Christians do die well."*

How well do you die? Most of us will never taste literal martyrdom, but we will all be invited to partake in a spiritual one. In our pain, we may try to circumvent this process. If we have a strong and controlling temperament, we may even try managing our own crucifixion. That is the ultimate manifestation of control issues! We may experience the emotions of anger, impatience, abandonment or despair. We may try to bargain our way out of our Cross of Surrender or try to scheme our way around it. We may also be tempted to lose heart. Everything within us resists going to this place. Ironically, the Cross is our only path to total inner healing. It is the threshold of something new.

"I have been crucified with Christ
and I no longer live, but Christ lives in me.
The life I live in the body, I live by faith in the Son of God,
who loved me and gave himself for me."
— Galatians 2:20

There is an old story of a monk, who under a vow of silence, was allowed to speak only two words per year. At the conclusion of the first year, he stood before his superior, the abbot, and chose his two words carefully: "Bed hard!" At the end of the second year, he spoke these two words to the abbot: "Food bad." The third year found him again standing before his superior. This time his final two words were: "I quit!" "Good!" the abbot shot back. "All you've done since coming here is complain, complain, complain!" More often than not, our times on the cross require us to hold our tongue, refuse to defend ourselves and rest in God's future vindication.

The meeting I had scheduled was going to be challenging. I was being asked to explain some of my past leadership decisions to some key leaders in our church. It was a necessary meeting to clear the air between us so that we could move on. To be honest, I was looking forward to it almost as much having as a root canal! Compounding this, I was in a place of some significant personal brokenness at the time. I felt vulnerable and weak, yet responding well to God's dealing was even more important to me than the issues being discussed. As I was praying about the meeting, God gave me a clear and vivid vision. What I saw was the rough wood grain of cut timber. What was remarkable was that it was an up-close view, as if I were looking at it from just an inch away. God's message to me was, ***"Sonny, here is your cross. Will you die well?"*** I knew that God had orchestrated all of these events to help me experience, in part, my Cross of Surrender. It was an opportunity to die well. By His grace, I did. We had some very healthy, honest, non-toxic communication. They did not go on the attack and I did not sin by becoming defensive. That day our relationship experienced some real reconciliation and we have been able to move on together with great joy.

"I seem forsaken and alone, I hear the lion roar;
and every door is shut but one, and that is Mercy's door."
— William Cowper

Crucifixion is a dreadful way to die. Further, we cannot crucify ourselves alone - we need the grim help of others. Think about it in graphic terms: If you set out to literally crucify yourself, you would likely begin with your feet. Although excruciatingly painful, you could conceivably be able to drive the spike through both of your feet. Then you might stretch your left arm out, holding the second spike in that hand. With careful blows, you would be able to sink the nail through your hand and into the wood. The third and final nail becomes your problem. How would you fasten your right hand to the cross? This is where God uses others in our lives to help finish the job. Some of these may be your enemies; those who irritate us are very good with a hammer and nail. Most often, however, God will use our friends. The irony of this heightens our pain and bewilderment. We feel betrayed and misunderstood - but the job gets done.

> "If an enemy were insulting me, I could endure it;
> if a foe were raising himself against me, I could hide from him.
> But it is you, a man like myself, my companion,
> my close friend,with whom I once enjoyed sweet fellowship
> as we walked with the throng at the house of God."
> — Psalm 55:12-14

Time to Reflect...

DATE

How close are you to your Cross of Surrender?

What are some ways that you have tried to avoid your Cross?

NO.

DATE

How has the Cross of Surrender been applied to your soul?

What does it mean for you to become "like him in his death?" (See Philippians 3:10-11)

Cross Words

For as painful as it is, the cross is what we have in common with Jesus. He is our example for how to experience this stage of our journey. Once we recognize that God is in the midst of our Surrender, it can actually be a place of great transformation. If we do the soul work required by this stage, we will not recognize ourselves on the other side of the cross. The Gospels record seven distinct things that Jesus said from His cross. Each has great meaning for us, but I will highlight three in particular that help us to follow Christ's example of dying well.

1. "Father, forgive them, for they do not know what they are doing." – Luke 23:34

Because God uses others in our lives to complete our crucifixion, there will be people we must choose to forgive. One of my favorite things to do is to interview veteran saints about their passage from Stage Five to Stage Six. When I asked Pastor Jim Darnell to describe his key to handling this part of his journey, he said that it was his decision to forgive those who have hurt him over the years. It matters not whether they were right or wrong in their actions, what matters is our response. As my father-in-law, Denver Jones, used to say about this kind of pain, "It will make you bitter or better." We will not move on successfully from Stage Five unless we deal with the bitterness and unforgiveness in our hearts.

2. "My God, my God, why have you forsaken me?" – Mark 15:34

The darkness of ultimate spiritual surrender can be overwhelming. We can feel like God and others have forgotten us in our greatest hour of need. With great anguish we cry out to God, *Why do you allow this to continue? Haven't*

I suffered enough? At times we can even feel abandoned by God. Our spirit is void; we feel alone and forsaken. Can you pause to imagine the prolonged spiritual tension as Jesus shouted this prayer to His Father from the cross? There was no answer, no voice from heaven, no miraculous deliverance. This same question is formed on our lips when we are facing Surrender of soul. Many of David's psalms were written from this place of anguish of soul. They offer us some rich prayers to help our perspective.

3. "Father, into your hands I commit my spirit." – Luke 23:46

This was the final statement of Jesus before breathing His last on the cross. It is a prayer of ultimate surrender. While it does not precede literal death for us, it does speak of an absolute letting go of self-preservation. We have already come to realize the limitations of our body and soul. Now all we have left is our spirit to relinquish to God. Something deeply spiritual shifts when we come to this place. It marks the beginning of something new.

> "Let us fix our eyes on Jesus, the author and perfecter of our faith,
> who for the joy set before him endured the cross, scorning its shame,
> and sat down at the right hand of the throne of God.
> Consider him who endured such opposition from sinful men,
> so that you will not grow weary and lose heart."
> — Hebrews 12:2-3

In his great Christian classic from 1670, the French archbishop and author, François Fénelon, writes: "Many think that dying to themselves is what causes them so much pain. But it is actually the part of them that still lives that causes the problem. Death is only painful to you when you resist it. Your imagination exaggerates how bad death will be. Self-love fights with all of its strength to live. Die inwardly as well as outwardly. Let all that is not born of God within you die."

Die Well

Well, my dear fellow traveler, how are you doing? There is nothing elegant or easy about applying the cross to our lives. Surrender can be a slow process as God pries our fingers loose one at a time. The fact is we die to both good and bad at the cross. Our vices as well as our virtues must go to the place of ultimate surrender. Only on the other side of the cross are these restored to our life with Christ's imprint. The challenge for our unsurrendered will is to die well. God uses the cross not to eradicate our soul, but to transform it.

A true sign of our progress, in this place of Brokenness, is the ability to look at our painful and confusing experiences with the eyes of the patriarch, Joseph. After being sold as a slave by his brothers and enduring the excruciating mistreatment in Egypt, he was able to see God's bigger plan unfolding in it all. Listen to what Joseph says to his brothers as they reunite: ***"You intended to harm me, but God intended it for good to accomplish what is now being done, the saving of many lives"*** (Genesis 50:20). Through our experiences of brokenness, God moves to redeem all things. We must cease defending ourselves and grant forgiveness to our offenders in order to live in God's eternal purpose. When we can come to this gracious perspective, it is evidence that we are ready to embrace our cross.

Make no mistake about it; this is not light stuff. Some travelers find the Cross of Surrender too much to bear and retreat to prior stages or pull into the parking lots. This greatly lessens the work of God through them. I hope better things for you. Look, I think I see a light on the road ahead; let's get closer and see if it will guide us on in our journey.

Going the Second Mile

Read Psalm 131. Use this psalm to ask God to bring you the grace you need to surrender.

Listen to the song "Lay It Down" by Jaci Velasquez and make it your personal prayer.

Read the following quote from Charles H. Spurgeon and consider your "inward poverty." Do you avoid it or find the King there?

> "Quietude, which some men cannot abide because it reveals their inward poverty, is a palace of cedar to the wise, for along its hallowed courts the King in His beauty [stoops] to walk."
> 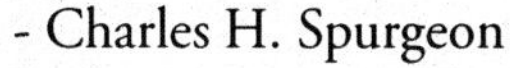
> - Charles H. Spurgeon

Read the Christian classic, The Seeking Heart by Fenelon (SeedSowers Publishing) and let his message help you in your "dying well".

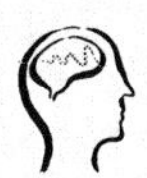

Memorize Luke 9:23-24. Consider what "your cross" looks like in practical terms.

To help you find forgiveness for your offenders, read The Bait of Satan by John Bevere (Charisma House)

Read the lyrics for the 1896 hymn "I Surrender All" by Judson Van DeVenter. Consider how you may surrender those "hold out" areas of your life to Christ.

Stage 5 – "Surrender" Highlights

Strengths:

- The grace to surrender our will
- Entering into the sufferings of Christ
- Being weak so that Christ is strong

Weaknesses:

- Wanting to fast-forward the process
- Anger, resistance and bargaining
- Impatience and loosing heart

Moving On:

- "Father Forgive Them..."
- "My God, why have You forsaken me?"
- "Into Your hands I commit my spirit."

Life Stage Axiom:

- "Die Well"

Notes

"Character cannot be developed in ease and quiet. Only through experiences of trial and suffering can the soul be strengthened, vision cleared, ambition inspired, and success achieved."

— Helen Keller

9

Coming Into Your Spacious Place

Stage Six: "Authenticity"

"I will be glad and rejoice in your love,
for you saw my affliction
and knew the anguish of my soul.
You have not handed me over to the enemy
but have set my feet in a spacious place."
— Psalm 31:7-8

"It's like I've been asleep for decades and woke up in a new world...a world with a new purpose and values. When I look back on my prior years from this perspective, I see how asleep I was to so much around me. God has used this awakening to redirect my life. The things that used to be gods to me no longer have a pull on me. Instead of being self-centered, I am God-centered and others-centered."

"Through my recent struggles, I have come to know myself and accept myself in all of my strengths and weaknesses. I have fully forgiven myself and my offenders. In fact, I see the fingerprints of God on my past trials and I thank Him for them."

"All I know is that I am Father's little child. To be loved by Him and to love Him are my greatest joys. I will do whatever He asks me to do. I find that He leads me to serve others in the simplest ways."

"My time with God, reading His Word and listening to His Spirit is so rich now. Before, I used to rush through my devotions; now it is my very lifeline! I never knew how intimate this time could be. It has totally rearranged my life."

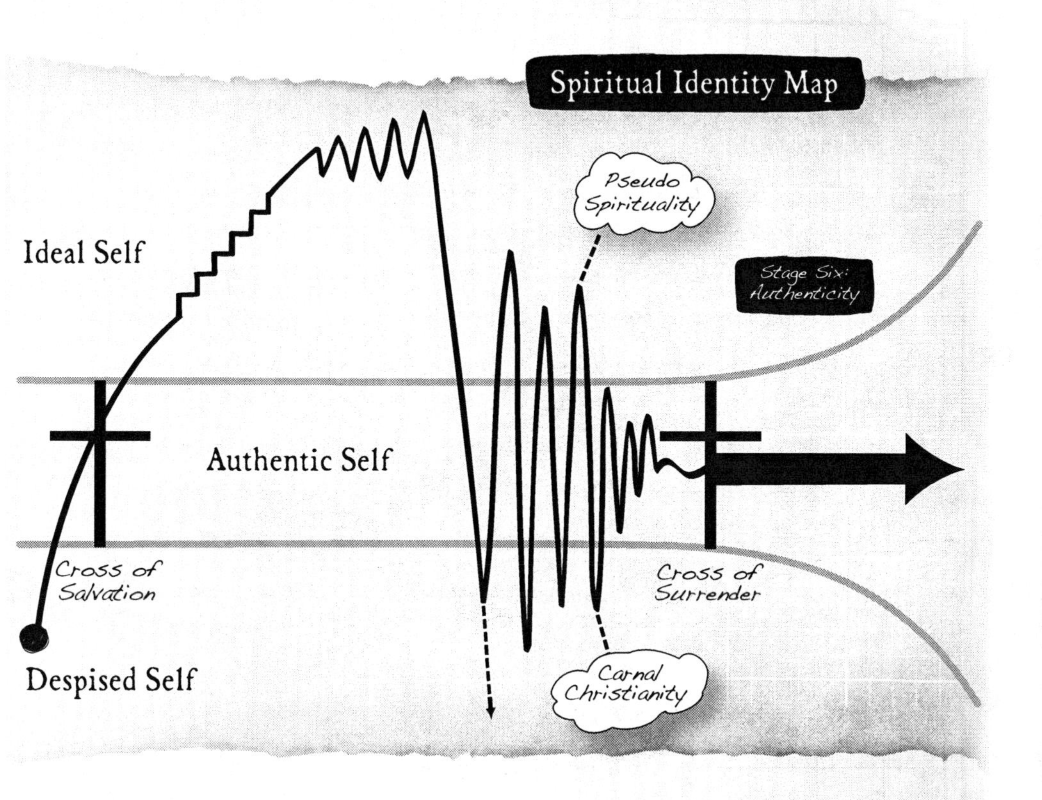

The dawning of Stage Six Authenticity brings us into a place of great freedom and peace. In contrast with the two preceding stages, this is a place of renewal. It is like crossing a desert wasteland and discovering an oasis with palm trees for shade and a spring-fed pool for refreshment. This is the *"spacious place"* that King David wrote about in the above passage from Psalm 31.

Notice on the map that the lines of our Authentic Self actually broaden out like the bell of a trumpet. This is to illustrate the opening up of new realms of personal discovery and ministry. Our Authentic Self seems to broaden out in every direction. The highway is wider than It has ever been for us. There is no longer a need to reach beyond our Authentic Selves. Through the dying process of the cross, God has actually brought forth a new life! Those things we once longed for in our Ideal Self, now come to us more easily and in a richer dimension. Also, as strange as it may seem, some of the realms of our Despised Self that we jettisoned as inappropriate now return to our lives. This is not a regressing to the transgressions of our past, but a new-found freedom to live in the Spirit and go places without sinning. What used to feel like walking a tightrope for Jesus now feels like a superhighway of holiness (Isaiah 35:8). This is a difficult concept to describe because it can be easily misunderstood for spiritual permissiveness. However, if the Cross of Surrender has done its deep work in us, the broadening road is place of Spirit-led fruitfulness. It's a winsome holiness that knows how to both stand to expound the deeper dealings of God and roll on the floor with the kids. A suspiciously "unknown author" said, "The mark of a successful person is one that has spent an entire day on the bank of a river without feeling guilty about it."

"Let's just go ahead and be what we were made to be,
without enviously or pridefully comparing ourselves with
each other, or trying to be something we aren't."
— Romans 12:5, The Message

The Authentic Self that we began to discover in Stage Four Brokenness is now our life's reality. This brings a whole new potential we never dreamt possible. There is both a *focus* and a *freedom* that comes to us in this place. We can live in the tension of both *rest* and *reaching*, of *peace* and *passion*. Our soul finds a life-giving balance in this stage. We discover how potent it is to be uniquely *us* in God and we joyfully leverage it to bear greater fruit for Him. Here, we've decided that we are not retiring, we are re-firing! There is an intensity that comes to our lives not based on the *drive* of our soul but the *depth* of our soul. This intensity was formed by the pruning process of God in our lives. With some of our former trappings trimmed away, we are free to discover who we are called to be and what we are to do in God's Kingdom. At this stage, we come to see that God's purpose for us fits hand-in-glove with our uniqueness. It was there all along. We were just too active, too inflexible or too successful to see it. Here we can be our *Authentic Selves* in the shadow of our own cross—now all is grace!

Dr. Henry Cloud in his book *Integrity* says it this way, "People who do best in life have a well-defined identity on a number of fronts. They are secure in their boundaries, they know what they like and don't like, what they believe in and value, and they love and hate the right things. They are not wishy-washy and what psychologists call identity diffused, wondering who they are or what they are about, or thinking that they are everything. You get a good definition of who they are just from being around them."

When I was a young hard-charging pastor out to do something great for God, I had the privilege of meeting Pastor John Carr, a Welshman who lived in Dundee, Scotland. He spoke with a rich brogue that demanded attention. Pastor Carr was in his seventies when we met. He was spry and sharp and loved to walk. I remember walking with him around a three mile lake and peppering him with questions about ministry, church life and the Kingdom of God. As a Stage Three Warrior, I wanted to gain all the spiritual combat savvy I could from this battle-scarred veteran. While he gave me some helpful insights, the thing I remember him saying most throughout our conversation is, "Sonny, all I know is that I am Father's little child." This stunned me and did not seem to fit into my arsenal of useful ministry advice. Now I realize that dear brother John was speaking out of his life stage. He had great experience and fruit in ministry, but God had brought him to a very simple place of contentment - being loved and cared for by the Father. I was face-to-face with Authenticity and didn't know it!

Life in this new spacious place is only possible because of the character God has formed in us. It has uniquely equipped us to survive in the atmosphere of Stage Six. It is like an astronaut preparing for a space walk. If he or she attempted to leave the spacecraft without the proper spacesuit, their body would not be able to survive. But if the astronaut dons the proper spacesuit and goes through the proper procedures, they are able to do something very few people get to enjoy...walk in outer space! Similarly, this place of Authenticity is only designed for those who have been properly molded by life's journey. There are no shortcuts on the Spiritual Identity Map that lead to Authenticity. Only submitting to God's dealings while walking through our life stages will produce the character and soul formation that makes it possible to enjoy this new expanse. In losing ourselves, we have found our true selves.

Stage Six Authenticity finds us relating to others in a new way. We are more understanding and compassionate of people. We no longer try to "fix" others with our knowledge or power. Instead, we are prone to being more sympathetic listeners who respect their place on the journey and the accompanying hidden workings of God. In the past we were self-oriented; now, as life veterans, we are others-oriented.

Our perspective in life has changed. It is broader than it was before. We are more committed to God's Word and will than ever, but now we hold it with more love and understanding. God is bigger to us than we could have ever grasped before. His ways are more transcendent than we once perceived. Our view of life through the toilet paper tube has changed to looking through the narrow end of a funnel and realizing that there is a vast expanse out there – more than we could ever grasp! Serving God's purpose on earth is our passion and focus. We realize that life is short and no longer are we inclined to live for our own ends. The Bible gives King David one of the greatest compliments one could ever receive about the way he lived:

"For when David had **served God's purpose** in his own generation, he fell asleep [died]; he was buried with his fathers and his body decayed."
— Acts 13:36

Just Another Day in Paradise

As we have learned in our journey together, each life stage holds its own strengths as well as its own unique weaknesses and temptations; this stage is no different. On the other side of the Cross of Surrender, we feel that we have been squeezed through a knothole. Having endured that wrenching experience, we are now tempted to pull off to the side of the road for a rest. The problem comes when our rest stop becomes our *rest home!* Let's face it; our emotions have been stretched, our soul has been tried, our will has been broken. Somehow we have survived. We are weary and the temptation to go into spiritual retirement sets in. Spiritually speaking, we want to sell our house up North and move to Arizona to play shuffleboard and drink iced tea all day. Friend, nothing could be more devastating to God's plan for your life! Those who do life well are a rare treasure; like fine wine – they improve with age. What a shame it is to see a "fine wine veteran" pour their life down the drain of self-serving mediocrity!

"For we are God's workmanship, created in Christ Jesus to do good works, which God prepared in advance for us to do."

— Ephesians 2:10

God has a "to do" list which He has drawn up for each of us. He gives us this brief life span to fulfill those good works. However, life veterans can fall into the trap of using our sense of freedom selfishly. At the very time we are best suited to pour into others, we choose retirement mode! There's also the lie of thinking, *"They don't want to hear from me. What do I have to offer?"* We can get caught up living in our past instead of investing in others' futures. The truth is, younger and less experienced travelers need us; they need to hear the wisdom and balance we've found. How sad it would be to enter heaven with our "to do" list only half completed!

"The black cloud which hangs over many a dying brow
means the stain of an influence lost for Christ."
— Henry Drummond

In Joshua 14 we read an amazing story about Caleb during the conquest of the Promised Land. As you may remember, Joshua and Caleb were among the twelve spies who scouted out the Promised Land. It was God's intent to lead them right into the land without the forty year wandering. However, ten of the spies came back with the report that the land contained giants and walled cities. The people became frightened and thought it too difficult to conquer. Joshua and Caleb, however, gave a different report: "We should go up and take possession of the land, for we can certainly do it" (Numbers 13:30). The people of God balked at God's opportunity and what began as a picnic by the river turned into forty years of a bad camping experience!

Forty-five years later, Caleb, who was now in the twilight years of his life, speaks to Joshua, the commander of Israel. Look at this man as he embodies all the renewed zeal of Stage Six Authenticity! He says to Joshua, "So here I am today, eighty-five years old! I am still as strong today as the day Moses sent me out; I'm just as vigorous to go out to battle now as I was then. Now give me this hill country that the LORD promised me that day. You yourself heard then that the Anakites were there and their cities were large and fortified, but, the LORD helping me, I will drive them out just as he said" (Joshua 14:10-12). From a natural perspective, Caleb should have been slowing down and enjoying some of the Promised Land. Rather, we see him begging to drive giants out of the hill country! Can you see the potency of his Authenticity? He is a great example of one who honored God fully in his earlier life stages and because of that reaped the benefits of abundance later in life!

Often, those living in true Authenticity can be misunderstood by people in earlier stages of life. For example, Stage Two Learners are confused by people in Stage Six because they are not dogmatic in their answers. Similarly, Stage Three Warriors may be frustrated by those in this stage because they do not exude the enthusiasm Warriors deem necessary. When Jesus took up the basin and towel to wash His disciples' feet, Peter was offended. Jesus replied, "You do not realize now what I am doing, but later you will understand" (John 13:7). Those walking in Authenticity are often judged by others with limited perspectives as being out of touch with reality. As Ralph Waldo Emerson said, *"To be great is to be misunderstood."*

In their book, *The Critical Journey,* Janet Hagberg and Robert Guelich write: "At this point in the journey, we let God be God from the inside out instead of the outside in. We let God direct our lives from a calm stillness inside, from a peace of soul and mind. We can be ourselves fully as fragile, spotty, incomplete, and imperfect, yet wise, loved, willing and called. It is a miracle to be able to let ourselves be used fully by God despite our shortcomings. In fact, God even fully uses our shortcomings. All are gifts to us."

"The real test of a man is not when he plays
the role that he wants for himself,
but when he plays the role destiny has for him."
— Vaclav Havel, the first president of the Czech Republic

Time to Reflect...

DATE

Who have you known that truly lives in Authenticity?

How have they impacted your life?

How has your perspective of God's purpose changed as you have journeyed?

Live to Give

Veteran missionary, Wayne Myers, has been inspiring hearts for world missions for nearly sixty years. With his gentle yet impassioned voice he would often proclaim his life message: "Live to give!" God wants this axiom etched on the heart of the Stage Six traveler. We must not forget that God has made a great investment in our lives and He wants to make some withdrawals. However, I want to warn you that this lifestyle is divinely countercultural. It means putting away our dream of spiritual retirement and living to invest in others. It means looking past our insecurities and perceived generation gaps to pour into others. It means becoming a Caleb!

Peter Drucker has observed that the life veterans among us have not proved to be the fertile source of volunteerism we had once expected. Instead, they tend to cut their engines off and lose their edge. He believes that if we do not seriously get in the game of serving others by age forty-five, and if we are not vigorously involved in it by age fifty-five, it will never happen!

Our fellow travelers in earlier stages desperately need us to model spiritual Authenticity. They need to see someone who has done life well by honoring God and managing their soul. We need to show them that there is life for them around the next corner. Their best days are yet ahead! It is alarming to see how many young people have grown cynical so early in life. They have lost hope; they no longer dream. Too often, they have given up on Christ and His Church. Stage Six leaders, we need you to rise up with zeal and unfold the map for us! The last prophet of the Old Testament gives us a sobering admonition for our generation when he said, "See, I will send you the prophet Elijah before that great and dreadful day of the LORD comes. **He will turn the hearts of the fathers to their children, and the hearts of the children to their fathers;** or else I will come and strike the land with a curse" (Malachi 4:5-6).

"Give me a young man in whom there is something of the old,
and an old man with something of the young; guided so, a man may
grow old in body, but never in mind."
— Cicero (De Senectute, XI)

Perhaps the most refreshing aspect to Authenticity is that of loving Christ and others more deeply. It is a beautiful thing to see someone in Stage Six with fresh water still coming out of their well. They have not allowed hurt, misunderstanding, setbacks and grief to poison their soul. My late father-in-law, Denver Jones, was this way. He would wake up in the morning singing and praising God. Even in his eighties you could find him getting excited about God, skipping a step, doing a little leap and shouting, "Glory!" He wasn't putting on airs; he was being freely authentic in his love for God.

"The righteous will flourish like a palm tree, they will grow like a cedar
of Lebanon; planted in the house of the LORD, they will flourish in the
courts of our God. They will still bear fruit in old age, they will stay fresh
and green, proclaiming, 'The LORD is upright; he is my Rock,
and there is no wickedness in him.'"
— Psalm 92:12-15

If this is your home stage in life right now, I would encourage you to live to give. Pour out your love to God and others. Do not go into spiritual retirement. Tell us your stories; we need you! The Apostle Paul spent the final season of his life in Authenticity. As he invested in Timothy, Titus and others, he left a legacy for all of us to enjoy. We see the fullness of his heart coming through in his final letter to Timothy:

"For I am already being poured out like a drink offering, and the time has come for my departure. I have fought the good fight, I have finished the race, I have kept the faith. Now there is in store for me the crown of righteousness, which the Lord, the righteous Judge, will award to me on that day."

— 2 Timothy 4:6-8

Well fellow traveler, we have been on quite a journey together. I trust that our Travel Guide, the Holy Spirit, has spoken to you about your current home stage. But *knowing* where we are on the map is only part of our task! Don't stop here; that would be like buying a new car without putting enough gas in it to drive it home! The next chapter will offer some significant insights to help us stay fueled up for our journey. I look forward to exploring them with you!

Going the Second Mile

How have you found the principle of 2 Corinthians 1:3-5 to be working in your life?

> "Praise be to the God and Father of our Lord Jesus Christ, the Father of compassion and the God of all comfort, who comforts us in all our troubles, so that we can comfort those in any trouble with the comfort we ourselves have received from God. For just as the sufferings of Christ flow over into our lives, so also through Christ our comfort overflows."

Search www.godtube.com for "The Journey Israel Hanna" - the life story of Israel (Jim) Hanna. Watch the 20 minute video story of Mr. Hanna's life and identify all six developmental stages.

Memorize Acts 20:22-24 for a proper perspective on Stage Six Authenticity.

Read the following quote from Henry David Thoreau and share with someone how this describes Stage Six on the Spiritual Identity Map.

> "If one advances confidently in the direction of his dreams, and endeavors to live the life which he has imagined, he will meet with a success unexpected in common hours. He will pass an invisible boundary; new, universal, and more liberal laws will begin to establish themselves around and within him; and he will live with the license of a higher order of beings."

There is a rabbinical saying: "God will one day hold us each accountable for all the things He created for us to enjoy, but we refused to do so." What are some of those things that God has given you to enjoy?

Read the lyrics for the well-loved hymn "It is Well With My Soul" by Horatio G. Spafford. This hymn was written after two major traumas in Spafford's life. The first was the great Chicago Fire of October 1871, which ruined this wealthy businessman financially. A short time later, while crossing the Atlantic, all four of Spafford's daughters died in a collision with another ship. His wife Anna survived and sent him the now famous telegram, "Saved alone." Several weeks later, as Spafford's own ship passed near the spot where his daughters had died, the Holy Spirit inspired these words. Identify how God is bringing you to a place where you can truly say, no matter what the circumstance, "It is well with my soul."

Stage 6 – "Authenticity" Highlights

Strengths:

- *Richness of Christ-like character*
- *Others-oriented & compassionate*
- *New perspective of God's eternal purpose*

Weaknesses:

- *Going into "spiritual retirement"*
- *Use your new freedom selfishly*
- *Live in your past, not in others' futures*

Moving On:

- *Live to give out of God's investment in you*
- *Model spiritual authenticity*
- *Love Christ and others deeply*

Life Stage Axiom:

- *"Live to Give"*

Notes

"On earth we are wayfarers, always on the go. This means that we have to keep on moving forward. Therefore be always unhappy about where you are if you want to reach what you are not. If you are pleased with what you are, you have stopped already. If you say; 'it is enough,' you are lost. Keep on walking, moving forward, trying for the goal. Don't try to stop on the way, or to go back, or to deviate from it."

— Saint Augustine

"There's no arrival unless there is a plan to go."

—John Cassian

10 Finding Your Way

What You Need to Thrive on Your Journey

"Above all else, guard your heart,
for it is the wellspring of life."

— Proverbs 4:23

Like learning the "rules of the road" when driving, it is important to learn some of the basic principles of navigating the Spiritual Identity Map. Let's review some truths about life stages:

1. One stage is not better or "more spiritual" than the other, each has its appropriate time in our lives.
2. We tend to place ourselves further ahead on the map than we actually are.
3. The stages are cumulative; each builds upon the others preceding it. We have a Home Stage, but can visit our past stages.
4. We tend to look down on those in earlier stages and misunderstand those in later stages.
5. Understanding some aspects of a particular stage is not the same as experiencing it. Finding your Home Stage has more to do with actions and attitudes rather than insight and observations.

So, what if you have read through the map and have yet to determine your Home Stage?

This could mean that you are in the process of transitioning from one stage to another or that you are stuck in one stage. It could also mean that you are in one of the "parking lots." The following charts will help you to further identify where you are on the map.

Stage One: New Life

Characterized By:	Awakening, spiritual new birth, relief, excitement, innocence
Biblical Character Example	Philippian jailer - Acts 16:25-34
Strengths	Freedom, forgiveness, awe of God, wonder, new life purpose and meaning
Weaknesses	Sense of unworthiness; over-dependant on feelings, unaware of God's Word and ways, not fully leaving old life
Life Stage Axiom	"Celebrate Grace"

Stage Two: Learner

Characterized By:	Discovery, gaining insight and experience, digging deeper, sense of rightness
Biblical Character Example	The Bereans - Acts 17:11 and Psalm 119
Strengths	Learning identity in Christ, hunger for God's Word, love for family of God
Weaknesses	Judgmental of others, "us against them" mentality, knowledge without wisdom
Life Stage Axiom	"Learn All You Can"

Stage Three: Warrior

Characterized By:	Achieving, leading, conquering, attaining, solving, building, protecting
Biblical Character Example	James and John - Mark 10:35-39; Luke 9:51- 56
Strengths	Accomplishing spiritual goals, zeal and vision, buoyant in spirit and faith
Weaknesses	Spiritual pride, self-strength, addicted to fruit-bearing, insensitive to the hurting
Life Stage Axiom	"Go For It"

Stage Four: Brokenness

Characterized By:	Uncertainty, feeling out of control, confusion, despair, depression, looking for escape
Biblical Character Example	Peter denying Christ - Luke 22:60-61
Strengths	Learning to embrace weakness, humility, gaining compassion for others
Weaknesses	Giving up on God & others, escapist behaviors, cynicism, categorizing our past as a waste
Life Stage Axiom	"Hang On, Don't Give Up"

Stage Five: Surrender

Characterized By:	Weakness, stillness, unknowing
Biblical Character Example	Esther - Esther 4:16
Strengths	Broken self-will, sharing in the sufferings of Christ, becoming weak so that Christ is strong
Weaknesses	Wanting to speed up the process, anger, resistance, bargaining, losing heart
Life Stage Axiom	"Die Well"

Stage Six: Authenticity

Characterized By:	Wisdom, being settled in identity, simplicity, loving devotion to God and others
Biblical Character Example	The Apostle Paul - Acts 20:34, II Timothy 4
Strengths	Richness of Christ-like character, being others-oriented, compassionate, gaining life perspective
Weaknesses	Using your new freedom selfishly, "spiritual retirement," living in the past
Life Stage Axiom	"Live to Give"

One Life Cycle or Many?

After studying the Spiritual Identity Map you may be asking yourself, *How many times do I have to go through this? Do I experience the stages one time in my life or do they keep repeating many times throughout my life?* In the West, we tend to have a more linear view of things in straight lines and progressive steps. The Eastern mind-set has a more cyclical approach to life. Let's look at how this applies to what we have learned in the Spiritual Identity Map.

There is a spiritual pattern woven throughout both the Old and New Testament. We also see it at work in nature, relationships, spiritual development and many other realms. It is the three-phase pattern of: Life, Death and Resurrection. Christ Jesus demonstrated the ultimate reality of this law when He came as a man, died on the cross and was raised to life by God's power. This pattern is God's redemptive loop woven into everything around us. This

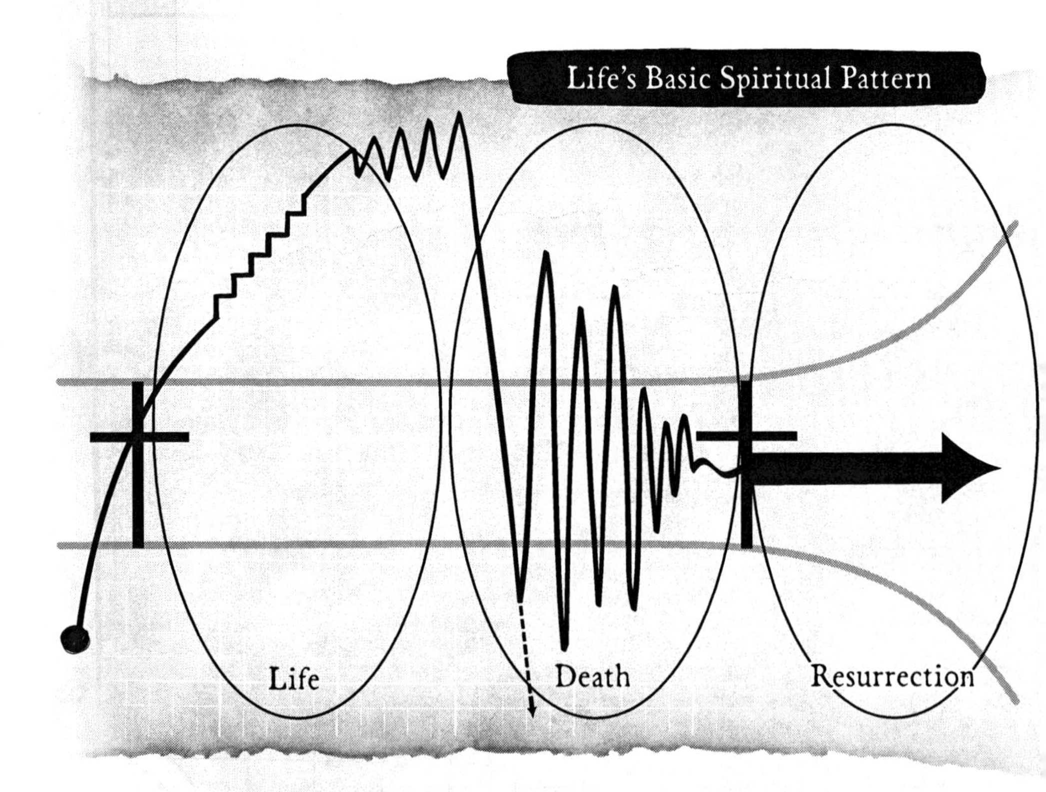

three step pattern is how we came to Christ and is how we continue to grow in Him. In a much broader view, Life, Death and Resurrection are the three basic stages of our life experience. Here it is overlaid on the Spiritual Identity Map.

Beyond the three basic stages shown above, I believe that our lives are also ***micro-cyclical*** in nature. This means that they hold many little cycles of life, death and resurrection. The Spiritual Identity Map shows us an overall picture of our predominant life cycle, yet throughout our life journey there are many experiences of Life – Death – Resurrection which God uses to continually transform us. These micro-cycles ↻ become the very nature of our spiritual development. This is illustrated in the map below.

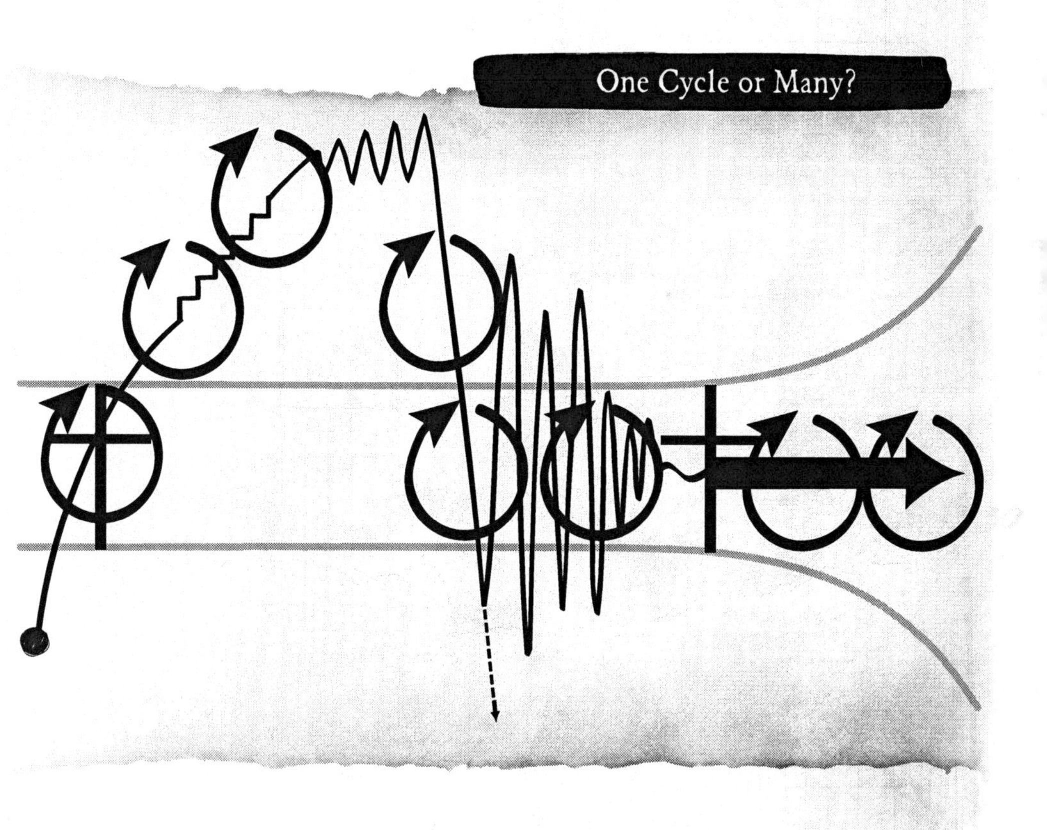

While our lives are micro-cyclical in nature, those cycles follow a larger life experience. This can make it difficult for someone to identify their place on the map. For example, a person in Stage Two may think that they have experienced the Brokenness of Stage Four when in reality they have simply experienced the Death phase of a micro-cycle. Further, even though a person has come through Stage Five Surrender, they will continue to experience these micro-cycles throughout their lives.

"The Christian, already God's by right of creation and by right of redemption,has yet again to become God's by virtue of his own free surrender of himself. And this self-surrender has, of course, to be continually repeated."
— C.E.B. Cranfield

Principles for Progress

The Apostle Paul gave us the proper way to think about our spiritual progress when he wrote to the Philippians:

"Not that I have already obtained all this, or have already been made perfect,
but I press on to take hold of that for which Christ Jesus took hold of me.
Brothers, I do not consider myself yet to have taken hold of it.
But one thing I do: Forgetting what is behind
and straining toward what is ahead,
I press on toward the goal to win the prize for which
God has called me heavenward in Christ Jesus.

All of us who are mature should take such a view of things.

And if on some point you think differently, that too God will make clear to you.

Only let us live up to what we have already attained."

— Philippians 3:12-16

This verse has always brought me both challenge and comfort. The Apostle Paul was obviously serious about fulfilling God's goal for his life. This meant a purposed, onward progression as well as a refusal to stop or get stuck. His prize in Christ was the all-consuming drive of his life. Then he challenges us by saying that this mentality is normative for those who are spiritually mature. He asserts, "All of us who are mature should take such a view of things." This "view" is that of pressing ever onward in Christ.

Yet, there are so many times we must be reminded, encouraged, instructed and prodded along on our journey. I am comforted by the promise that if at any point I should think differently about my spiritual progress, God will make it clear to me. Do you see Paul's confidence as he trusts the Holy Spirit to be his Travel Guide? We must hold the ground we have already attained in Christ while pressing on to new heights. Thankfully, God has promised to finish what He has started in us.

"When one door closes, another opens; but we often look so long and so regretfully upon the closed door that we do not see the one which has opened for us."

— Alexander Graham Bell

Now that we know about the six stages on the map, let's look at some timeless principles for progress.

1. **"Stuckness" is possible at any stage of our journey.** Traveler beware! Getting stuck is most often a slow and subtle reality. Fear, insecurity, unwillingness, laziness or growing comfortable in our current state are some of the reasons we do not move on in life. Comfort is a good thing, but can become a vice when we wrongly assume it will last forever. It causes us to lose our motivation to move forward. We may look back at our life and be pleased with the ground we have covered so far, but as the financial advisors often say, "Past performance does not guarantee future profitability." A willing and ready "yes" toward God is the best way to keep us from getting stuck.

2. **Times of movement can be scary** because we are transitioning into the unknown. The great patriarch, Abraham, demonstrated his faith in God when he left Ur at God's command. He set out for the land of promise not knowing where he was going. His example of faith gives us a picture of what it feels like to "believe God" when we have more questions than answers. It is this kind of faith that we need during transitions to overcome the feelings of insecurity and fear.

   Walking is a good analogy for our progress on the Spiritual Identity Map. Each step requires us to manage a certain amount of imbalance. If we examine the typical walking stride in slow motion, there is a point at which our body is literally teetering on the toes of one foot! Fearing this awkward position could keep us from making progress. Moving through the life stages is much like this. Between each stage is a natural point of imbalance and vulnerability. Sometimes we don't manage these steps well and end up on our rear end (spiritually speaking.) Picture a one-year-old learning how to walk. They barely become steady standing in one place on both feet before they are faced with the challenge of walking. Each step leaves them balancing on one foot while trying to figure out what to do with the one that is in the air. Fear of the unknown must never deter us from taking new steps on our journey!

3. **We cannot move ourselves;** God moves us as His timing and grace meet our cooperative response. Progress in Spiritual Identity Development holds a measure of divine mystery. It is a mixture of divine intention, human response, spiritual revelation, emotional maturity, life experiences and just raw grace! While we should apply ourselves to God's dealings, we cannot rush His process. Through defiance, we can slow, stunt and stall our progress to the next stage. Remember the principle of progress we discussed earlier: God's invitation followed by human response equals spiritual movement. This puts us in a watchful place of trusting in God for His direction. Proverbs 3:5-6 says, "Trust in the LORD with all your heart and lean not on your own understanding; in all your ways acknowledge him, and he will make your paths straight."

4. **Crisis often provides the energy for movement** from one stage to another. I think It is safe to say that most of us are crisis averse! We will avoid it if at all possible. Yet these experiences are the very fuel that God uses to propel us on in life. It has been observed that some very young people have a spiritual depth that defies their years. Upon exploration, we often find they have allowed God to use a crisis (or series of crises) to deepen their spiritual well. When we experience such things as losing a job, having to move, a devastating divorce, losing a loved one or enduring an illness, we are driven to find God's grace at a whole new level. Some spend so much time trying to discern the source

of their adversity (the devil, God, self or the world) that they miss the significance of their adversity. Transitions are tough, as are the emotions that come with them, but they are the necessary stuff of spiritual progress.

5. How well we are living our current life stage largely determines our success in the one to come. This principle for progress cannot be overestimated! For example, if a Stage Three Warrior learns to put down their sword, they will more readily submit to the disciplines of Stage Four Brokenness. Similarly, if a person in Stage Four Brokenness finally learns to surrender their selfish ambition to Christ, they will deal much better with the stillness of soul required by Stage Five Surrender. How we end our days is guided by the quality of the decisions we have made throughout our lives. If we hope to finish well, we must deliberately seek God's guidance and grace throughout each stage.

Proverbs 5:11-14 paints a vivid picture of how someone who did not do life well comes to the end of their days:

> "At the end of your life you will groan, when your flesh and body are spent. You will say, "How I hated discipline! How my heart spurned correction! I would not obey my teachers or listen to my instructors. I have come to the brink of utter ruin in the midst of the whole assembly."

So, how do we make sure that we are doing well in our current stage? I believe that we should be *stewards* of our current stage and *students* of our next stage. In other words, dig into the opportunities afforded you in your current life stage. Do not apologize for it or miss it altogether by wishing you were in a different one. God has us in this unique season to learn, grow and be fruitful. If we minimize our life, look over the fence or feel sorry for ourselves, our preparation for the next stage will be stunted. Success in serving God's purpose is achieved by fully applying ourselves to the realities of the immediate while being open to His leading into our future.

6. Relationships have potential to greatly help or hinder our progress on the journey. One of the benefits to understanding the Spiritual Identity Map is being able to appreciate other people in their place on life's journey. We learn to be more compassionate and less critical of those in different stages. We can understand the stages which we have been in; we are discovering our current Home Stage, and can only dimly conceptualize the stages yet ahead of us. Having friends who are in a variety of stages will help us gain a broader perspective. Living life with people who are self-aware in their journey will serve as both a mirror and stimulus for our soul.

Wise friends are also vital to help us stay accountable and on track. A circumspect traveler will follow the principle of *Two Hands and a Heart.* This principle looks like this:

Left Hand: Find a mentor who is in a later stage.

Right Hand: Be a mentor to one in an earlier stage.

Heart: Grow in the strengths of your Home Stage.

"A friend is one to whom you can pour out the contents of your heart, chaff and grain alike, knowing that the gentlest of hands will take and sift it, keep what is worth keeping and with a breath of kindness, blow the rest away."

— George Eliot

Where Are You?

By now you should have a pretty good idea of your Home Stage on the Spiritual Identity Map. Take a pen and draw a stick figure of yourself on the appropriate place on the map below. Next, identify someone on your "Left Hand" and "Right Hand" with whom you can discuss your journey. Draw them on the map in their life stage and label them with their names. I challenge you now to connect with them in a meaningful way to discuss their journey and learn from one another.

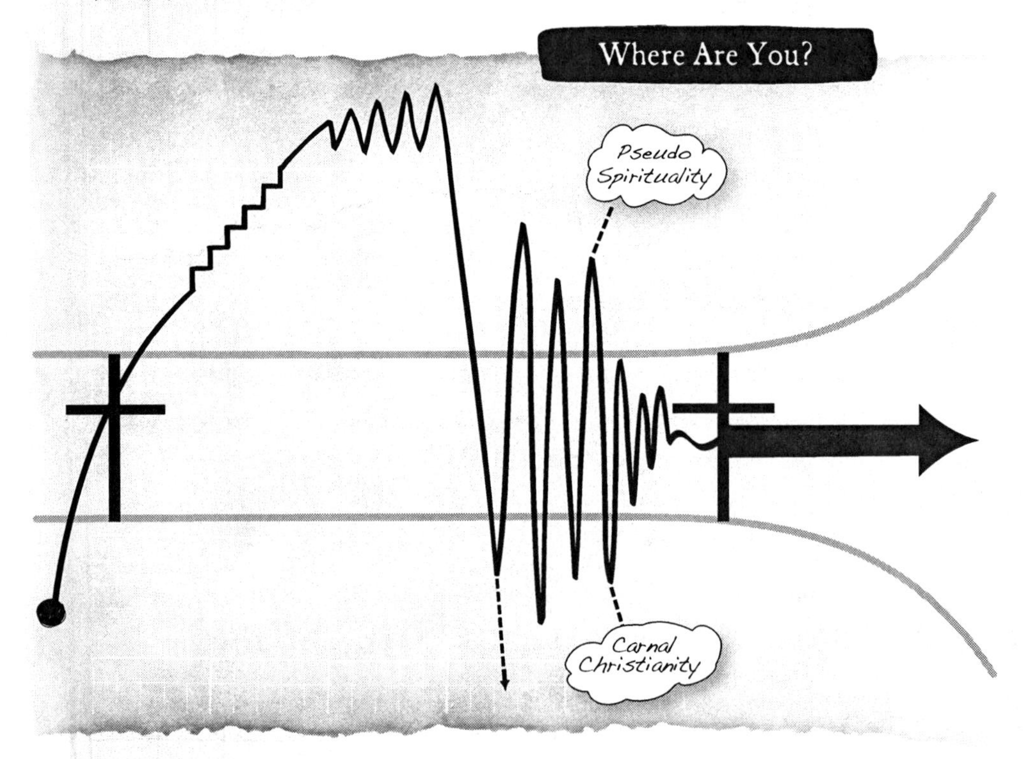

The next chapter offers many helpful insights to further understand specific aspects of your spiritual identity development process. I encourage you to spend time examining the ten life span studies. May God grant us His wisdom and grace as we serve Him on our amazing journey through life!

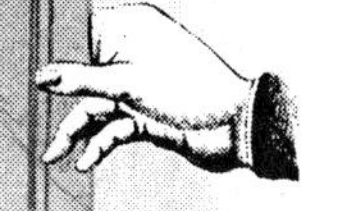

Going the Second Mile

Now that you know where you are currently on the map, consider how well you "served God's purpose" in each of the life stages you have experienced up to this point. In the space provided, give yourself a grade (A, B, C, D or F) based on how fruitful your time was in that stage. Place a "N/A" on the line if you have not yet been to that stage. Now discuss your assessment with a friend.

Life Stage Grade

Stage One – "New Life" ______

Stage Two – "Learner" ______

Stage Three – "Warrior" ______

Stage Four – "Brokenness" ______

Stage Five – "Surrender ______

Stage Six – "Authenticity" ______

A = Excellent

B = Good

C = Average

D = Needs Improvement

F = Poor

In the space below write a prayer to God telling Him how you want to navigate this time in your journey.

Watch the movie, Mr. Holland's Opus and observe his trials and triumphs through each stage of the journey. Note how well he ends his life as a result of making right choices.

Internet search the lyrics for the hymn "Have Thine Own Way, Lord" by Adelaide A. Pollard. Sing it or read it to the Lord as your life prayer.

Notes

"I used to ask God to help me. Then I asked if I might help Him. I ended up by asking God to do His work though me."

— Hudson Taylor

"For many of us the great danger is not that we will renounce our faith. It is that we will become so distracted and rushed and preoccupied that we will settle for a mediocre version of it."

—John Ortberg

11

Scenic Overlooks

"We live by faith, not by sight. We are confident, I say,
and would prefer to be away from the body and at home
with the Lord. So we make it our goal to please him,
whether we are at home in the body or away from it.
For we must all appear before the judgment seat of Christ,
that each one may receive what is due him for the things done
while in the body, whether good or bad."

— 2 Corinthians 5:7-10

Our journey has taken us through some amazing terrain. Now that we have visited each of the life stages and understand their contribution to our life, we can pull off the road to enjoy some breathtaking views! We will look at ten specific perspectives which I refer to as Scenic Overlooks. Each overlook will offer its own lessons in a specific aspect of life. There are many insights to be gleaned as we examine the progression of our soul using the Spiritual Identity Map. Many of these insights touch all six life stages and are helpful to look at from a bird's eye view. Let's pull over and take in some of these vistas.

Scenic Overlook One – Life Stages and Ages

Determining life stage is not truly a matter of age, but of how we have walked with God through life and responded to His dealings. However, this Overlook seems to be a general trend of Spiritual Identity Development as we get older. Keep in mind this is only a guide to assist us in thinking about our place on the map. The danger in applying approximate ages to our journey is that we can assume that we are at a particular stage solely due to our age. However, we have learned that our Spiritual Identity Development can be either stunted or enhanced due to many factors. The writer of Hebrews asserts: "though by this time you ought to be teachers, you need someone to teach you the elementary truths of God's word all over again" (Hebrews 5:12). With this in mind, please use this Scenic Overlook as simply a general guide based on my observations of individuals on their life journeys.

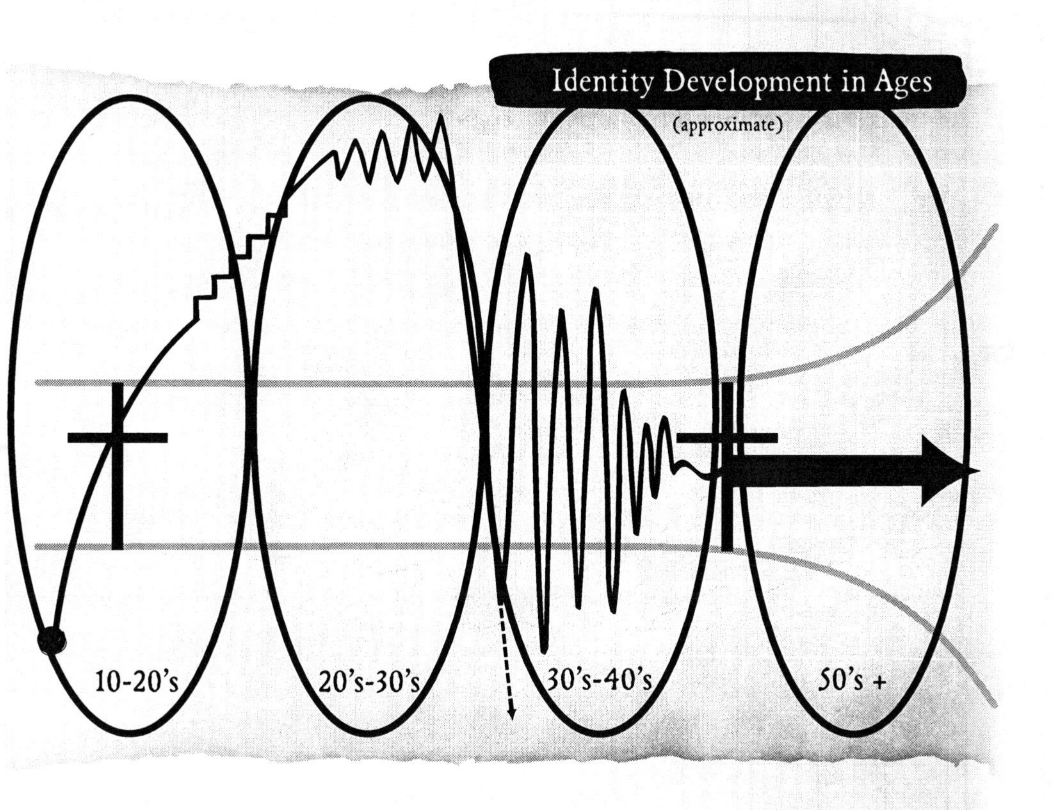

"Don't let anyone look down on you because you are young,
but set an example for the believers in speech, in life,
in love, in faith and in purity."

— 1 Timothy 4:12

"Young men, in the same way be submissive to those who are older. All of you, clothe yourselves with humility toward one another, because, 'God opposes the proud but gives grace to the humble.'"

— 1 Peter 5:5

Scenic Overlook Two – Wisdom and Zeal

It is beautiful to see the zeal and strength of youth. It spurs us on to new levels and requires us to think outside the box. Young people are often revolutionaries who are not afraid to challenge the status quo. We need them to be this way! They provide the rocket fuel for many great Kingdom endeavors. If you are in the early stages on the map, never apologize for your zeal…we need it!

"Never be lacking in zeal, but keep your spiritual fervor, serving the Lord." — Romans 12:11

"It is fine to be zealous, provided the purpose is good…" — Galatians 4:18

Similarly, wisdom is often what is seen among the older and more seasoned life veterans. Just as we need zeal to be released among our youth, we need this wisdom to be released among those in the later life stages. Wisdom is not merely worldly knowledge or "street smarts," rather it is the ability to rightly apply knowledge. It is divinely given as we acknowledge the will and ways of God.

"The fear of the LORD is the beginning of wisdom, and knowledge of the Holy One is understanding." — Proverbs 9:10

"I write to you, fathers, because you have known him who is from the beginning." — 1 John 2:14

On the Spiritual Identity Map the progression of wisdom and zeal may look like this over a given life span:

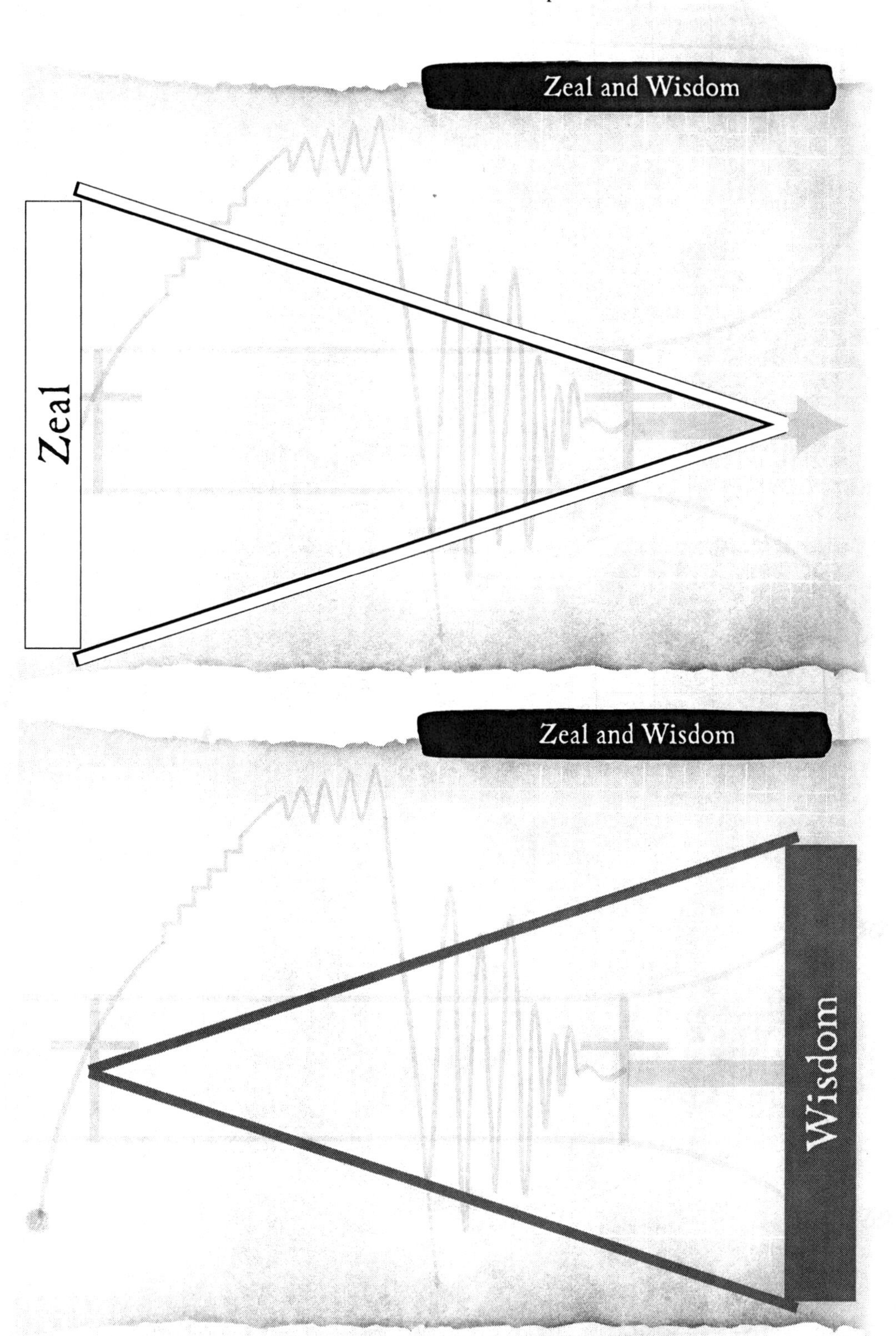
Zeal and Wisdom
Zeal
Zeal and Wisdom
Wisdom

It is typical to see zeal diminish and wisdom build as we age. However, this is not God's ideal. One of the lessons we can learn from the map is how to gain wisdom as a young person and find new zeal as we age. I believe that if we do life well, our whole journey can be marked by both zeal and wisdom. If the young received from the old and the old poured into the young we would see generations changed for God's glory. The very last verse of the Old Testament prophetically speaks to the power of this spiritual dynamic.

"He will turn the hearts of the fathers to their children, and the hearts of the children to their fathers; or else I will come and strike the land with a curse."
— Malachi 4:6

May God give us young people who are wise beyond their years and old people who display the zeal of youth! This ideal blend is illustrated below:

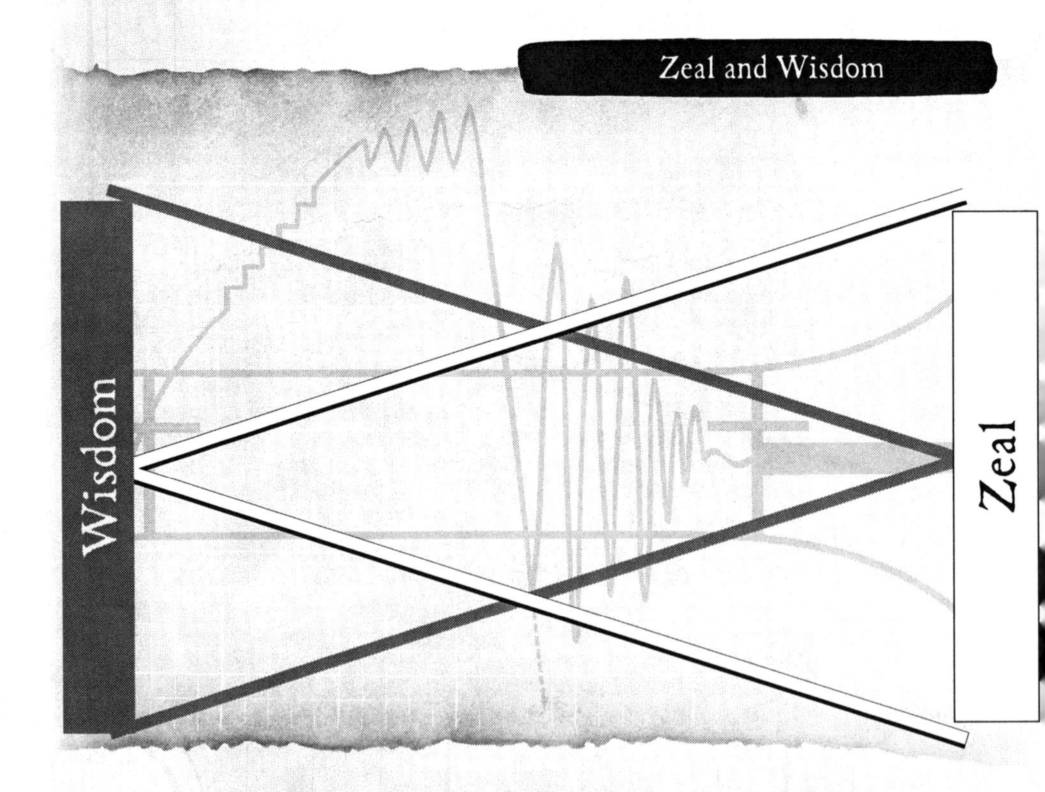

Scenic Overlook Three – The Life of the Apostle Peter

It is fascinating to study the lives of biblical characters in light of the Spiritual Identity Map. From them we glean great encouragement for our own lives. When we read of their triumphs in God, we are challenged to new heights. When we read of their failures, we are filled with hope that God can use one such as us! My favorite person to study in this regard is the Apostle Peter. He seemed to live his life stages to the extreme. Peter did not do anything half-hearted! This helps us relate to him and makes his passage through the life stages clearly visible.

The Life of the Apostle Peter

- From now on you will be catching men. –Luke 5:10
- He did not let anyone follow him except Peter, James, and John. – Mark 5:37
- But Peter declared, "Even if I have to die with you, I will never disown you. –Matthew 26:35
- And he went outside and wept bitterly. – Luke 22:62
- Simon, son of John do you truly love me more than these? –John 21:15
- I have prayed for you, Simon, that your faith may not fail. And when you have turned back, strengthen your brothers. – Luke 22:31-32

"Remember your leaders, who spoke the word of God to you. Consider the outcome of their way of life and imitate their faith."
— Hebrews 13:7

God worked in the life of the Apostle Peter to bring about significant transformation. We see this from his beginning as a rough-cut fisherman deeming himself "a sinful man," to the end of his life as a martyr for Christ. When Christ reinstated Peter after the resurrection, He simply asked him, "Peter, do you love me more than these?" When Peter answered in the affirmative, Jesus commissioned him to his high calling: "Feed and take care of my little sheep." In essence, Jesus was refocusing Peter's heart to find its expression in the tender nurture of the flock of God. Christ could now trust Peter with the shepherding of His sheep without concern that he would make lamb chops out of them!

Church history tells us that Peter died by being crucified upside down. This reveals the deep work accomplished in Peter's soul through the Cross of Surrender. The riveting account in The New Foxe's Book of Martyrs shows us Peter's transformation from an unworthy fisherman to a militant crusader and finally to a faithful shepherd …even to the point of death.

"Nero planned to put [Peter] to death. When the disciples heard of this they begged Peter to flee the city (said to be Rome) which he did after much pleading by the disciples. But when he got to the city gate he saw Christ walking toward him. Peter fell to his knees and said, 'Lord, where are you going?' Christ answered, 'I've come to be crucified again.' By this, Peter understood that it was his time to suffer the death by which Jesus had told him he would glorify God (John 21:19), so he went back into the city. After being captured and taken to his place of martyrdom, he requested that he be crucified in an upside down position because he did not consider himself worthy to be crucified in the same position as his Lord."

Scenic Overlook Four – The Life of Moses

Like the life of Peter, the life of Moses is also clearly seen in the Spiritual Identity Map. While Moses lived in the old covenant, not literally visiting the cross of Christ as we see in the New Testament, there are spiritual parallels we can draw from his life.

The Life of Moses

- God called to him from within the bush, "Moses! Moses!" – Exodus 3:4
- Moses said to the Lord, "O Lord, I have never been eloquent and I am slow of speech and tongue." – Exodus 4:10
- Moses said, "Let my people go." – Exodus 5:1
- Moses threw the tablets out of his hands, breaking them to pieces. – Exodus 32:19
- You will not bring this community into the land I give them. – Numbers 20:12
- Moses climbed Mount Nebo; there the LORD showed him the whole land. – Deuteronomy 34:1

"For everything that was written in the past was written to teach us, so that through endurance and the encouragement of the Scriptures we might have hope."

— Romans 15:4

Scenic Overlook Five – Life Perspective Changes

Passing through the stages of Spiritual Identity Development has a way of changing our perspective on life. These changes may be subtle or rather obvious, depending on our temperament and circumstances. For example, an optimist by nature may find themselves becoming quite pessimistic as they are walking through Stage Four. A realistic life perspective does not deny either our problems or the power of God to solve them. Having a realistic life perspective enables us to experience both with a confidence in God's sovereign control over all things.

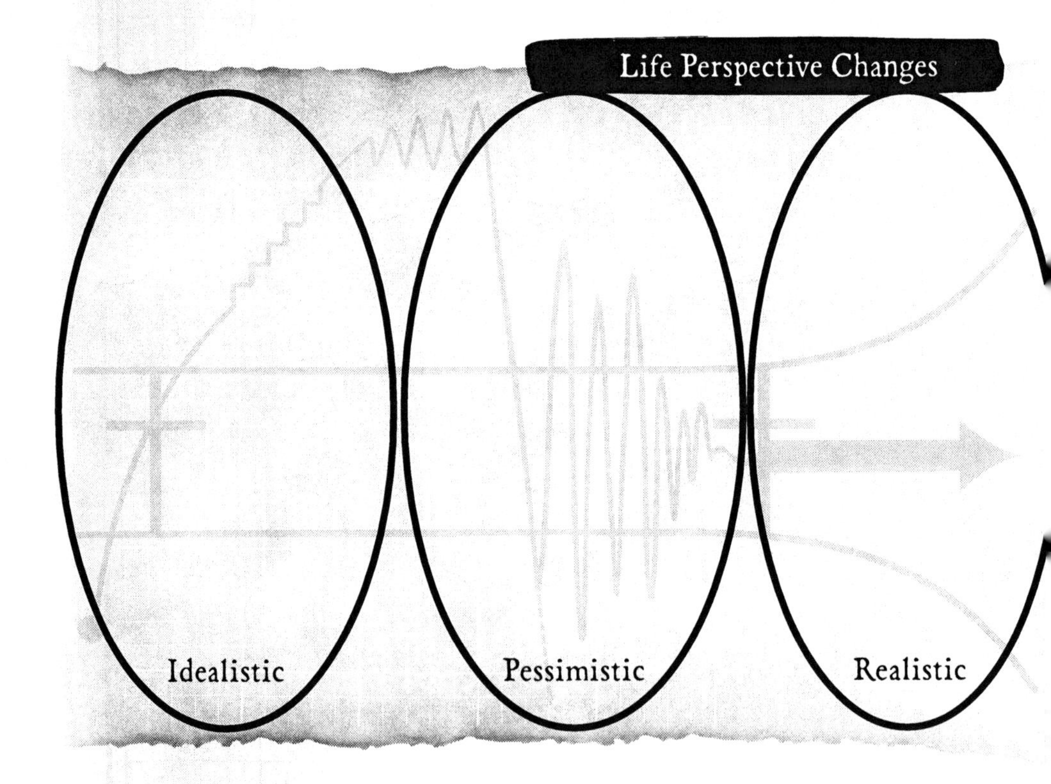

While each of us has been given a unique temperament from our Creator, we tend to view our environment based on the condition of our soul. The great Psalmist, King David, expresses a full range of emotion as he holds to faith through varied life experiences. Here are biblical examples of how these perspectives changed throughout his life. See if you can relate to any (and all) of them.

Idealistic Perspective:

"With your help I can advance against a troop; with my God I can scale a wall." – Psalm 18:29

Pessimistic Perspective:

"Save me, O God, for the waters have come up to my neck. I sink in the miry depths, where there is no foothold. I have come into the deep waters; the floods engulf me. I am worn out calling for help; my throat is parched. My eyes fail, looking for my God." – Psalm 69:1-3

Realistic Perspective:

"When I called, you answered me; you made me bold and stout-hearted. – Psalm 138:3

Scenic Overlook Six – Our Relationship with Jesus Christ

The Bible tells us that Jesus is "the same yesterday, today and forever" (Hebrews 13:8). However, our relationship with Him changes as we move through the life stages. He does not change, but our perspective of who He is and how He is working in our life changes.

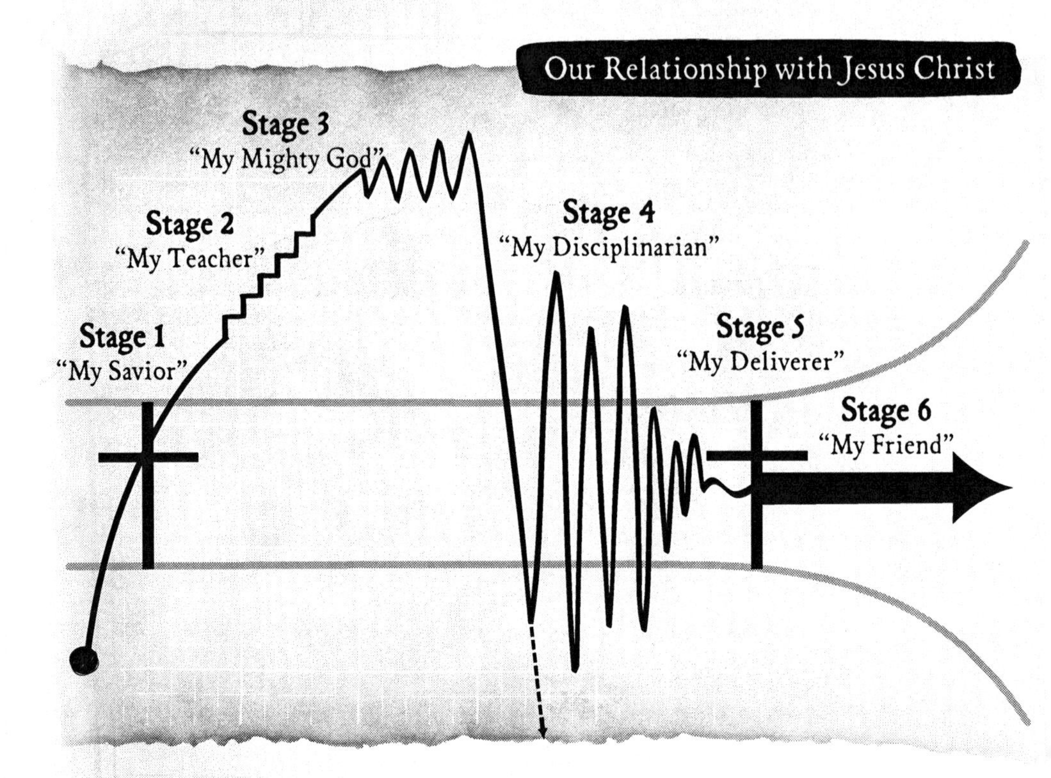

The Book of Revelation, for example, gives us a wide spectrum of how Christ is revealed. He is seen in Revelation 1:12-17 as the radiant "son of man." In Revelation 5:6-7 Christ is revealed as a "Lamb, looking as if it had been slain." And in Revelation 19:11-16 He is the conquering "King of Kings and Lord of Lords." Indeed, He is the magnificent and multifaceted Son of God! It will take us all eternity to discover the fullness of His glorious attributes.

While we experience Christ in many ways throughout our Spiritual Identity Development, there are general lenses we use in our different stages. This also helps us understand others in different places on the map as they experience Christ on their spiritual journey.

Scenic Overlook Seven – The View of Relationships

How we relate to other people tends to change as we go through life. Early on, we are dependent on those providing instruction regarding the Word of God. As Warriors, we tend to focus on what we are doing for God. In our later stages we rediscover the value of doing life with others in a more intimate and transparent way. Keep in mind that these are general trends and that they will blend throughout our journey. For example, the Apostle Paul was a very strong personality and he was used mightily by the Lord. It is interesting to study these three phases of how he related to others throughout his ministry:

Dependent

"After many days had gone by, the Jews conspired to kill him, but Saul learned of their plan. Day and night they kept close watch on the city gates in order to kill him. But his followers took him by night and lowered him in a basket through an opening in the wall. When he came to Jerusalem, he tried to join the disciples, but they were all afraid of him, not believing that he really was a disciple. But Barnabas took him and brought him to the apostles. He told them how Saul on his journey had seen the Lord and that the Lord had spoken to him, and how in Damascus he had preached fearlessly in the name of Jesus."

– Acts 9:23-27

Independent

"As for those who seemed to be important — whatever they were makes no difference to me;God does not judge by external appearance —those men added nothing to my message. On the contrary, they saw that I had been entrusted with the task of preaching the gospel to the Gentiles, just as Peter had been to the Jews.

– Galatians 2:6-7

Interdependent

"Do your best to come to me quickly, for Demas, because he loved this world, has deserted me and has gone to Thessalonica. Crescens has gone to Galatia, and Titus to Dalmatia. Only Luke is with me. Get Mark and bring him with you, because he is helpful to me in my ministry. I sent Tychicus to Ephesus. When you come, bring the cloak that I left with Carpus at Troas, and my scrolls, especially the parchments."

– 2 Timothy 4:9-13

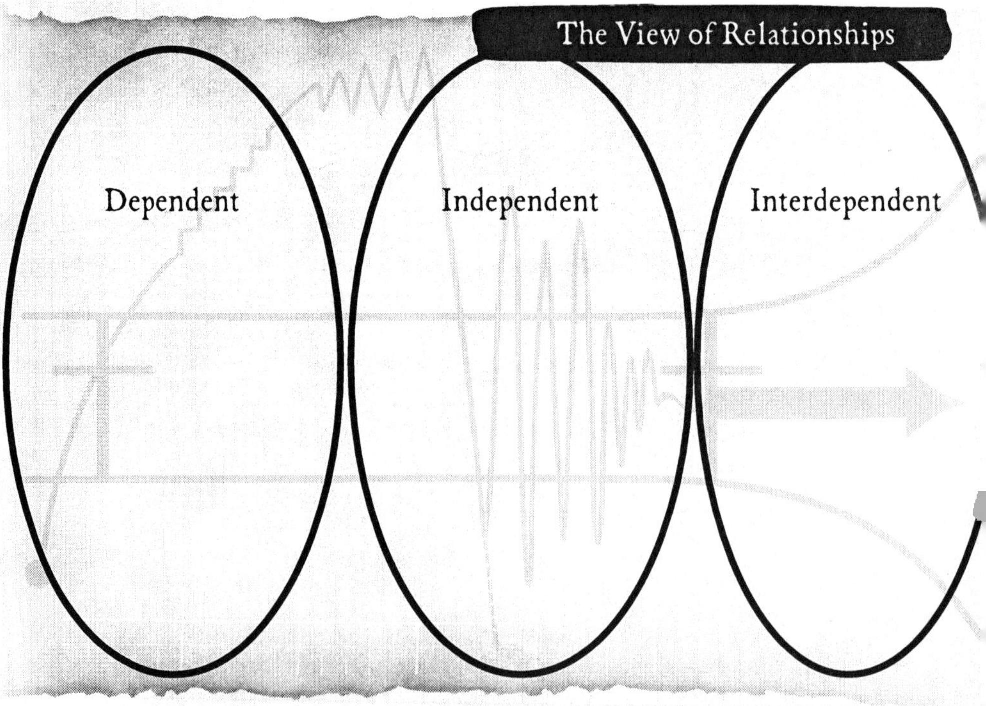

The View of Relationships

Dependent

Independent

Interdependent

Scenic Overlook Eight – The Marriage Relationship

As I discussed the Spiritual Identity Map with my wife, Becky, she made the observation that typical marriage relationships go through a very similar process. We enter marriage with an idealized view of how our lives will unfold. Somewhere along the line the shine wears off, reality sets in, and we have to do the hard work of becoming "one." (Genesis 2:24) Many become disillusioned at this point and begin looking for something to fill the void. They believe the lie that love is all about "that lovin' feeling." Infatuation is a fun and exciting season of a relationship, but it does not hold a candle to the depth and oneness of mature marital love! It is there, because of the hard work of oneness, that we hold a more accurate view of ourselves, our spouse and of God. Having allowed the love of God to satisfy the deepest needs of our soul, we are finally past ourselves and free to love and serve one another. Oh the joy! This view of the map illustrates some of our observations.

"Submit to one another out of reverence for Christ. Wives, submit to your husbands as to the Lord. For the husband is the head of the wife as Christ is the head of the church, his body, of which he is the Savior. Now as the church submits to Christ, so also wives should submit to their husbands in everything. Husbands, love your wives, just as Christ loved the church and gave himself up for her to make her holy, cleansing her by the washing with water through the word, and to present her to himself as a radiant church, without stain or wrinkle or any other blemish, but holy and blameless."

— Ephesians 5:21-27

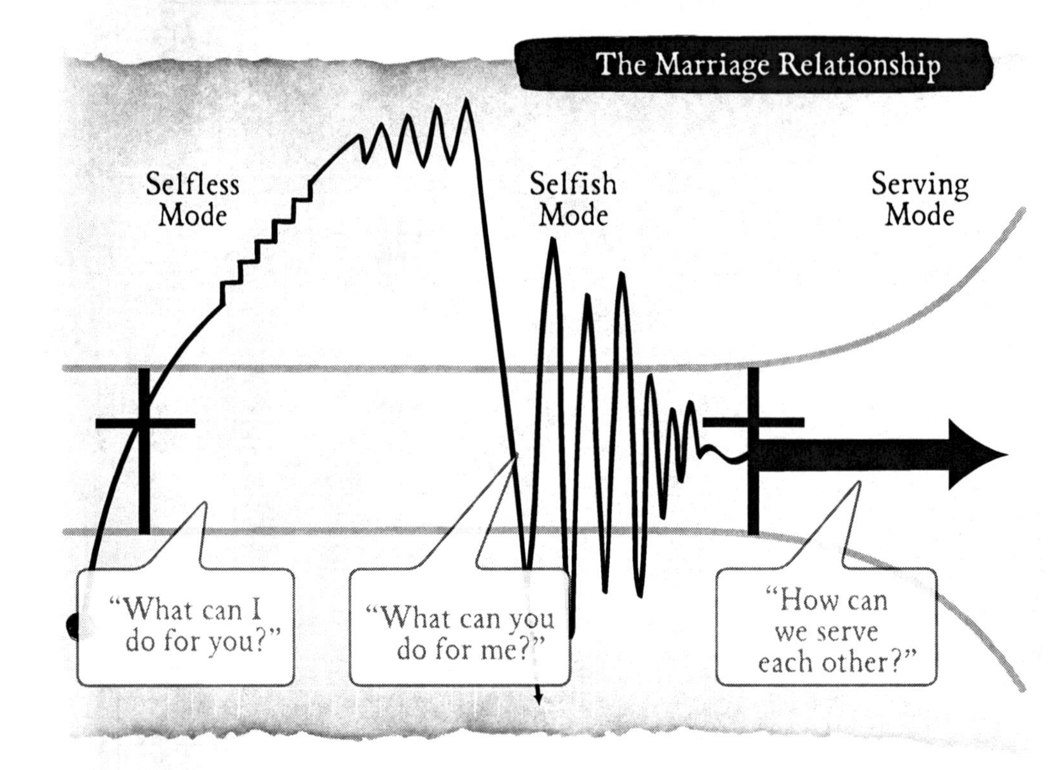

Scenic Overlook Nine – Our Values in Life

As we travel the Spiritual Identity Map, our values in life change because we are changing. This is not being fickle or insincere. Rather, it is God building different qualities in our lives as we move with Him. For example, the Stage Three Warrior values achievement and the same person in Stage Five Surrender values weakness. This is due to the inner, transformational work of God in our soul.

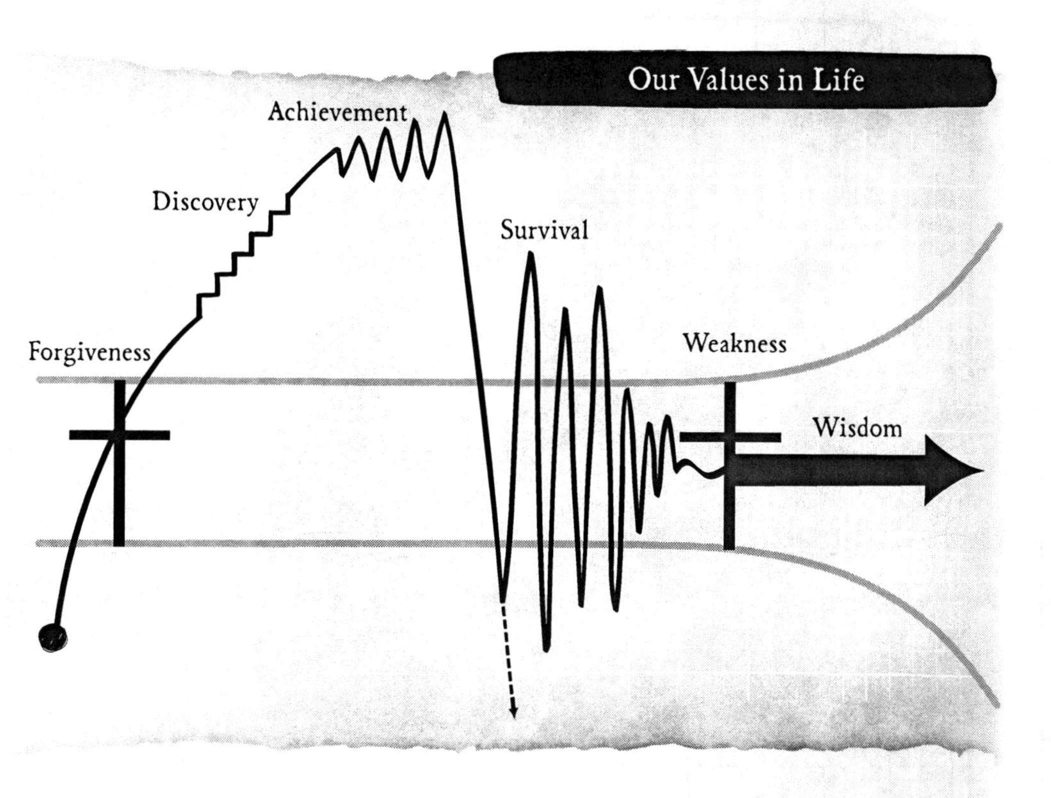

There is a time for everything, and a season for every activity under heaven...He has made everything beautiful in its time. He has also set eternity in the hearts of men; yet they cannot fathom what God has done from beginning to end.

– Ecclesiastes 3:1, 11-12

"The fear of the LORD is the beginning of wisdom; all who follow his precepts have good understanding.To him belongs eternal praise."

– Psalm 111:10

Scenic Overlook Ten – The Ministry of the Church

If the Church is going to truly be a redemptive community we must learn to minister to individuals at all six stages of their journey. I have observed that we seem to do better helping people on the first three stages than on the last three. Getting people saved, learning, and serving is what most church programs are designed to do. Many do that very well. However, I have come to call stages Four and Five "The Silent Stages" because they are not being addressed in most faith communities. Most people going through these difficult stages do not have words (or a theology) for what they are experiencing. The Silent Stages can be filled with shame and doubt – things that are not easy to speak about in most small group Bible studies. This void has left many churches filled with hurting and isolated people.

Lately, however, it has been refreshing to hear great Christian leaders talk and write about their personal ministry meltdown experiences. They have assured us that we are not alone and have given us some survival tips for navigating life in these seasons. Local churches can open up a great opportunity for ministry if they purpose to help people traverse the last three stages of Spiritual Identity Development. Below are some observations on what people need and what faith communities can offer at each new level of development.

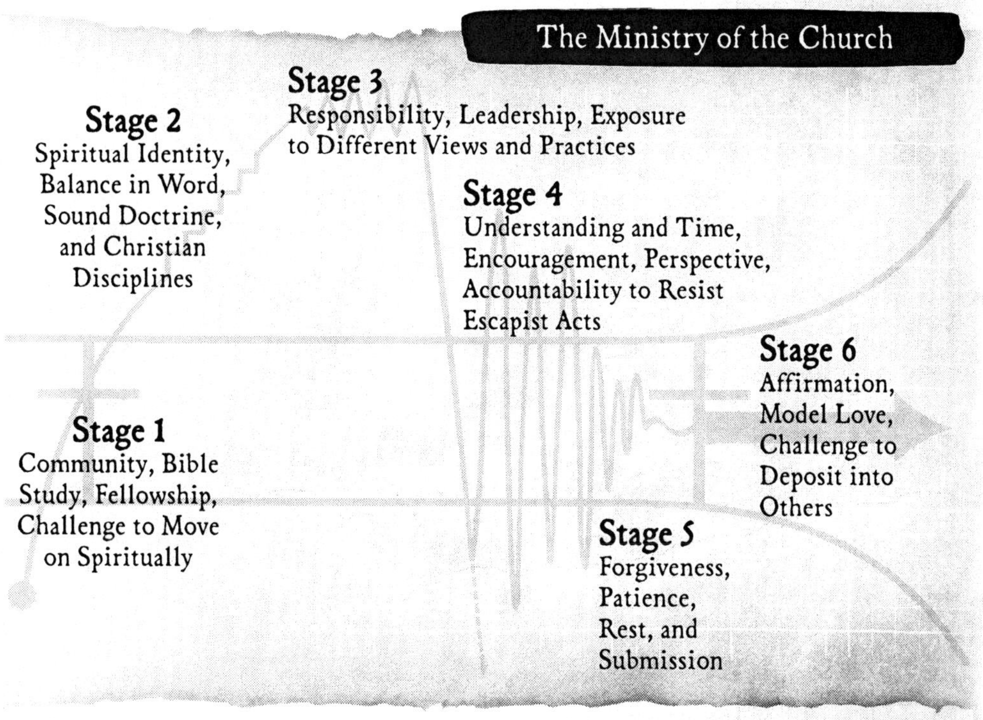

The Ministry of the Church

Stage 1
Community, Bible Study, Fellowship, Challenge to Move on Spiritually

Stage 2
Spiritual Identity, Balance in Word, Sound Doctrine, and Christian Disciplines

Stage 3
Responsibility, Leadership, Exposure to Different Views and Practices

Stage 4
Understanding and Time, Encouragement, Perspective, Accountability to Resist Escapist Acts

Stage 5
Forgiveness, Patience, Rest, and Submission

Stage 6
Affirmation, Model Love, Challenge to Deposit into Others

"It was he [Christ] who gave some to be apostles, some to be prophets, some to be evangelists, and some to be pastors and teachers, to prepare God's people for works of service, so that the body of Christ may be built up until we all reach unity in the faith and in the knowledge of the Son of God and become mature, attaining to the whole measure of the fullness of Christ."

– Ephesians 4:11-13

The Purpose of it All

The study of Spiritual Identity Development must never end with ourselves. The world is filled with thousands of "self help" books which are written from a self-centered or humanistic perspective. This is certainly the bent of human nature and our current culture. However, we are to be like King David, who "served *God's purpose* in his own generation" (Acts 13:36). We must be committed to something much bigger than ourselves! The calling of every Christian is to serve the unfolding, eternal purpose of God on earth. He is working through time and history to establish the centrality of Christ in all things (Ephesians 1:9-10; I Corinthians 15:24-28). This is the divine destiny toward which human history is marching. As believers, we have the privilege of cooperating with God in the unfolding of this divine plan!

Fellow traveler, we only have this one life to live for God. It is it said of King David that he served God's purpose in his generation and "**then he died…**" (Acts 13:36). The short life span given us on this earth is just a sliver in the vastness of God's timetable. We must be good stewards of our lives! Jesus has been victorious to bring us to a more abundant life (John 10:10). As the Westminster Confession states: "The chief end of man is to glorify God and to enjoy Him forever."

Our journey can be summed up in this descriptive passage:

"Therefore, since we are surrounded by such a great cloud of witnesses, let us throw off everything that hinders and the sin that so easily entangles, and let us run with perseverance the race marked out for us. Let us fix our eyes on Jesus, the author and perfecter of our faith, who for the joy set before him endured the cross, scorning its shame, and sat down at the right hand of the throne of God. Consider him who endured such opposition from sinful men, so that you will not grow weary and lose heart."

— Hebrews 12:1-3

God's will and His glory must remain central in our attitudes and actions if we are to properly navigate through our journey on the Spiritual Identity map. Those who have lived before us have paved the very road on which we are standing. They are cheering us on to the fulfillment of God's destiny for our lives. We must not give up! We must not be dissuaded! The journey takes us through some unbelievable ups and downs and ultimately leads to our Cross of Surrender and hopefully Authenticity. Our consolation is that Christ has trod this path before us and has gloriously triumphed!

We have seen much as we have traveled on this journey together. I pray that the unfolding of the map brought much clarity and confirmation to you. Knowing where you are on the map is affirming. Understanding others in their Home Stage will also enrich your relationships. You will be better at avoiding the Parking Lots. That great "cloud of witnesses" is in heaven cheering us on (Hebrews 12:1). Jesus has promised to be the Author and the Perfecter (finisher) of our faith. Let's trust Him at every level and keep our eyes on Him through it all.

"His divine power has given us everything we need for life and godliness through our knowledge of him who called us by his own glory and goodness."

— 2 Peter 1:3

Notes

FAQS

Q. Viewing life through stages seems a bit mechanical to me. Is this the best way to explore our developmental process?

Some people appreciate the life stage approach to personal development because it gives them a grid to understand themselves and others. Many people relate to the visual nature of the Spiritual Identity Map because it makes these sometimes vague principles easier to grasp. Understanding the developmental stages gives us a renewed appreciation for people in other life stages. I find that it actually can deepen our relationships. Individuals have also felt a strong clarity and affirmation come to them as they study the map. It puts things into perspective and gives them hope for their future development. Stage Four and Five travelers seem to really appreciate some understanding of what they are going through in a time that can be quite murky.

The weakness to the stage approach is that people can get so fixated on studying the stages that they miss the point of the journey all together. Some can take a rigid approach to their progress and see it as something to be "accomplished" rather than a journey to be experienced and savored.

Q. Is it possible for a devout Christian to skip the painful stages of Brokenness and Surrender and transition right into Authenticity? Don't Stages Four and Five demonstrate spiritual defeat and a lack of faith?

I remember being approached by a young man who asked this question at a conference where I had shared the Spiritual Identity Map. He took his finger from the peak of Stage Three and slid it smoothly down into Stage Six. It looked as if he were drawing a picture of the slow slope of the "Bunny Hill" at a ski resort! (I guess he wanted to avoid the "double black diamond" runs with all their peril and terror...you can't blame him.)

When someone in an early stage sees the dynamics of stages Four and Five they are often inclined to think that this wouldn't happen to them. It reminds me of the Apostle Peter's response to Christ after He told them that He was going to Jerusalem to suffer and be killed, "Never, Lord! This shall never happen to you!" The description of Stages Four and Five seem like something to be avoided at all costs. However, we must see these two important stages as gifts and graces from God. To deny them would be to deny a very real part of God's deeper work in our lives. What is worked in our soul through these stages is the very stuff that brings us to Authenticity. If a car was being built on an assembly line and a worker decided to skip the part where they put in the transmission, it wouldn't be very useful to the owner for the real work of driving.

Further, we must not see these stages as times of failure or backsliding. These stages are not reserved for a select few who need to have their inner lives rearranged. Sooner or later in life we come to realize that we, too, need to visit these places. No amount of hard work, sincerity, devotion or good behavior will exempt us from traversing the passages of Stages Four and Five. Are they difficult? Yes. Are they painful? Yes. Are they confusing? Yes, but they bring something to our lives that we could never receive if we were to gently glide over them and tenderly touch down in the land of Authenticity.

So, while we cannot skip these stages, we can do our best to cooperate with God through them. Remember, we cannot fast-forward through the stages, but we can painfully prolong them through resistance and unwillingness.

Q. Can a person be at more than one Home Stage at one time?

We will always have a predominant Home Stage, but there may be times when we feel like we are in more than one at the same time. This is likely due to a season of transition from one stage to another. We may also find it difficult to identify one distinct Home Stage because we are in the process of shifting from one stage to the next. Stuckness may also confuse our ability to identify a particular stage. We may have aspirations of being further along, but the reality is that our inner life and spiritual progress are stunted. Lastly, if we are given roles and responsibilities beyond our Home Stage, we may recognize that we are inwardly at an earlier stage yet outwardly trying to perform at a higher stage. This can bring great strain to our lives and likely will not be a sustainable way to live.

Q. Did Jesus Christ experience the Spiritual Identity Map as we do when He was a man on earth?

While it's not my purpose here to unfold an in-depth Christological treatise, we can examine what the Scriptures tell us about Christ's humanity. We must first understand that while Christ came fully as a man, He was the sinless Son of God (II Corinthians 5:21). In His perfection, Christ also experienced the full range of human emotions. When He was twelve years old it is said that he was obedient to Mary and Joseph and "**grew** in wisdom and stature, and in favor with God and men" (Luke 2:52). The writer of Hebrews tells us that "although he was a son, he **learned obedience** from what he suffered" (Hebrews 5:8). It's apparent that Christ developed as a person, learning through a process of inner and outward growth. When reading the gospels one can envision Him experiencing the realities of the developmental stages: New Life, Learner, Warrior, Brokenness, Surrender and Authenticity.

Unique from us, however, Christ was never deceived about His identity, although Satan aimed his temptations at that foundation. (Luke 4:3, 9) Christ did not have a "Despised Self" as He was sinless. He was never confused about his "Ideal Self" as we may be. I believe that Jesus lived in the realm of Authentic Self from His youth. From age twelve Jesus had a profound awareness of his identity and calling. This was seen when He told Mary and Joseph that "I had to be in my **Father's** house" (Luke 2:49).

While Christ took on our human nature in His incarnation, He did not take on our *sinful* nature. We are told that Christ "made himself nothing, taking the very nature of a servant, being made in human likeness. And being found in appearance as a man, he humbled himself..." (Philippians 2:7-8). Scripture affirms that "he had to be made like his brothers in every way, in order that he might become a merciful and faithful high priest in service to God" (Hebrews 2:14, 17). Throughout Jesus' life on earth He had a sense of the unfolding of seasons, often saying, "My time has not yet come" (John 2:4; 7:6; 8:20). Jesus knew what it was like as a man to submit His will to the will of the Father. Hebrews 4:15 tells us that He was tempted in every way as we are, yet without sin.

In light of these observations, I think that it is reasonable to conclude that Christ Jesus experienced the strengths and temptations concurrent with each life stage and sinlessly navigated through each one. In fact, it is the victory of His obedience that gives hope to every fellow sojourner!

Q. Why is some sort of "crisis" necessary for us to transition from one stage to the next?

Crisis is often used by God to get us moving along in our journey because we are creatures of habit. These crises can take a variety of forms: inward, outward, circumstantial, relational and directional. Individuals may also move ahead by a God-given hunger for more in their spiritual lives. We may also be helped to transition when we gain a new insight through an experience, a book, a minister, a friend or directly from the Spirit of God.

Q. Can a person move backward from their Home Stage into the stages they've already experienced?

Yes, there are a few reasons we may experience this dynamic. If we come to a point of resistance, pain or confusion in our journey we may retreat to more familiar ground to gain stability. Sometimes we may be thrust backward by unique demands upon our lives at given times. For example, we may be in Stage Four Brokenness and because of some new responsibilities be forced into a Stage Two Learner mode. Further, if we have been stuck for a long period of time and begin to move on again, Christ may guide us back through some of the foundational lessons of our earlier days.

Q. You addressed the Spiritual Identity Map from an Evangelical perspective. Do these principles of movement hold true in other branches of Christianity or even with non-religious people?

The stages of Spiritual Identity Development can be seen in the full range of Christian groups from Liberal to Conservative. While each has their own particular emphasis and value structure, we can observe individuals moving through the same stages of development. For example, a Conservative Stage Three Warrior might be passionate about evangelism while a Liberal Stage Three Warrior might be passionate about feeding the poor.

The non-Christian may relate to some parallel experiences in their natural course of life. This is because there are themes on the map that are common to human development. For the Christian, however, God is intimately involved in forming Christ-like character in us so that we can better serve His purpose on earth. The Cross of Salvation is our unique starting point. His Holy Spirit empowers us and guides us along our way. The Cross of Surrender goes deeper than mere human reformation; it is a spiritual experience. Jesus walks with us on this incredible journey that He alone walked in utter perfection.

Q. What about people who seem to die prematurely and without getting to finish their journey?

It is tragic to experience the death of those in the prime of life. I have officiated at the funerals for a number of young people and it is indeed heartbreaking. We don't have answers to all of the *"why"* or *"what if"* questions. We must trust in a totally loving and sovereign God at such times. I believe that God will reward us based on the time we had to experience life and respond to His will. We have seen how the untimely death of one can impact the lives of hundreds for good. The veil between heaven and earth is thinnest when we experience the death of a loved one. We come face-to-face with our own life's journey in light of eternal realities. The Holy Spirit wants to use this awakening to move us toward Christ.

Credits:

Introduction

"Know Thyself" actually predates Socrates, and is traditionally ascribed to one of the "Seven Sages of Greece." Socrates is reported to have quoted it from Thales, from whom the phrase likely originated.

Oscar Wilde (1854-1900) *The Soul of Man Under Socialism, Fortnightly Review,* February 1891

Joshua J. Heschel , *The Prophets* (New York, NY: Harper Collins, 1962) page 488

Chapter 3

"Just as I Am" written by Charlotte Elliott in 1835, music by William B Bradbury

Leonard Cohen, *The Spice-Box of Earth* (London, England: Jonathan Cape, Ltd, 1961)

John C. Maxwell, *The 21 Irrefutable Laws of Leadership* (Nashville, TN: Thomas Nelson, Inc., 1998), page 183

Chapter 5

Robert Bly, *Iron John* (Reading, MA: Addison-Wesley, 1990), page 146

John Dryden, (from his poem) "Johnnie Armstrong's Last Goodnight"

Bob Buford, *Half Time* (Grand Rapids, MI: Zondervan, 1994), page 65

Chapter 6

Robert Hicks, *The Masculine Journey* (Colorado Springs, CO: NavPress Publishing Group, 1993), page 106

Floyd McClung, *Finding Friendship with God* (Ann Arbor, MI: Vine Books, 1992) page 186

Abraham Lincoln, Letter to John T. Stuart, January 23, 1841 (*The Writings of Abraham Lincoln,* Volume 1, Abraham Lincoln research site, www.att.net)

Bill Hybels, *Courageous Leadership* (Grand Rapids, MI: Zondervan, 2002), page 193

Gary Thomas, *The Beautiful Fight* (Grand Rapids, MI: Zondervan, 2007), page 209

Parker Palmer, "Leader to Leader" Number 22, Fall 2001

Chapter 7

C.S. Lewis, *Screwtape Letters* (New York, NY: Harper-Collins, 2001)

Robert Hicks, *The Masculine Journey* (Colorado Springs, CO: NavPress Publishing Group, 1993), page 129

Arnold Toynbee, *A Study of History* (New York, NY: Oxford University Press, 1946)

Chapter 8

R. Somerset Ward, *To Jerusalem: Devotional Studies in Mystical Religion* (1931; reprint, Harrisburg,PA: Morehouse, 1994), pages 177-78

Janet Hagberg and Robert Guelich, *The Critical Journey* (Salem, WI: Sheffield Publishing Company, 2005, 1995)

Charles R. Swindoll, *Laugh Again* (Dallas, London, Vancouver, Melbourne: Word Publishing, 1992)

François Fénelon, *The Seeking Heart* (Christian Books Publishing House, 1992), Page 13

Chapter 9

Eugene Peterson, *The Message* (Colorado Springs, CO: NavPress Publishing Group, 1993, 2002), Romans 12:5

Dr. Henry Cloud, *Integrity* (New York, NY: Harper-Collins, 2009), page 144

Henry Drummond, *The Greatest Thing in the World: and 21 other Addresses* (London: Collins, 1953), page 236

Janet Hagberg and Robert Guelich, *The Critical Journey* (Salem, WI: Sheffield Publishing Company, 2005, 1995), page 140

Bob Buford, *Half Time* (Grand Rapids, MI: Zondervan, 1994), page 111

Chapter 10

C.E.B. Cranfield, *The Epistle to the Romans,* (Edinburgh: T&T Clark, 1979), page 600

Chapter 11

John Foxe, *The New Foxe's Book of Martyrs,* Rewritten and updated by Harold J. Chadwick (Gainesville, FL: Bridge-Logos Publishers, 2001) page 7

About the Author

R. Sonny Misar was born into a Christian home in 1963 and raised in suburban Chicago, Illinois. As a teen, he began to hear God's call on his life. He attended Liberty Bible College in Pensacola, Florida where he graduated with honors earning a Bachelor in Theology with a Minor in Counseling.

Having been in pastoral ministry since 1986, Sonny carries a passion to equip believers to experience the power of God from the inside out. While pastoring in Winona, Minnesota, he travels nationally and internationally strengthening pastors, leaders and local churches to fulfill their God-given calling.

Sonny has been married to Becky since 1987 and is blessed with four Jesus-loving children: Natalie, Jodi, Erin and Scott. He also serves on the National Leadership Team of *Ascension Fellowships International,* an apostolic network of churches in the United States.

For more information, group study resources, or to inquire about scheduling a *Journey to Authenticity* speaking engagement with Pastor Misar at your church or event, please go online to our web site at:

www.journeytoauthenticity.com